The Thinker's Library, No. 7

AUTOBIOGRAPHY
OF
CHARLES DARWIN

WITH TWO APPENDICES,
COMPRISING A CHAPTER OF REMINISCENCES
AND A STATEMENT OF CHARLES
DARWIN'S RELIGIOUS VIEWS,

BY HIS SON,

SIR FRANCIS DARWIN
(Fellow of Christ's College, Cambridge)

LONDON:

WATTS & CO.,

5 & 6 JOHNSON'S COURT, FLEET STREET, E.C.4

Originally published in 1929 by the Thinker's Library

This edition published in the UK in 2003
by Icon Books Ltd., Grange Road,
Duxford, Cambridge CB2 4QF
E-mail: info@iconbooks.co.uk
www.iconbooks.co.uk

Published in the USA in 2003
by Totem Books
Inquiries to: Icon Books Ltd.,
Grange Road, Duxford,
Cambridge CB2 4QF, UK

Sold in the UK, Europe, South Africa
and Asia by Faber and Faber Ltd.,
3 Queen Square, London WC1N 3AU
or their agents

Distributed to the trade in the USA by
National Book Network Inc.,
4720 Boston Way, Lanham,
Maryland 20706

Distributed in the UK, Europe, South
Africa and Asia by TBS Ltd., Frating
Distribution Centre, Colchester Road,
Frating Green, Colchester CO7 7DW

Distributed in Canada by
Penguin Books Canada,
10 Alcorn Avenue, Suite 300,
Toronto, Ontario M4V 3B2

Published in Australia in 2003
by Allen & Unwin Pty. Ltd.,
PO Box 8500, 83 Alexander Street,
Crows Nest, NSW 2065

ISBN 1 84046 503 4

Printed and bound in the UK by
Mackays of Chatham plc

CONTENTS

PUBLISHERS' NOTE

WITH the kind permission of Messrs. John Murray and the approval of the family of Charles Darwin, this volume is reprinted from the *Life of Charles Darwin*, edited by his son, Sir Francis Darwin.

First published in the Thinker's Library, **1929.**
Second Impression, **1931.**

AUTOBIOGRAPHY OF CHARLES DARWIN

[My father's autobiographical recollections, reproduced here, were written for his children,—and written without any thought that they would ever be published. To many this may seem an impossibility; but those who knew my father will understand how it was not only possible, but natural. The autobiography bears the heading, *Recollections of the Development of my Mind and Character*, and ends with the following note :—"Aug. 3, 1876. This sketch of my life was begun about May 28th at Hopedene,[1] and since then I have written for nearly an hour on most afternoons." It will easily be understood that, in a narrative of a personal and intimate kind written for his wife and children, passages should occur which must here be omitted ; and I have not thought it necessary to indicate where such omissions are made. It has been found necessary to make a few corrections of obvious verbal slips, but the number of such alterations has been kept down to the minimum.—F. D.]

A GERMAN Editor having written to me for an account of the development of my mind and character with some sketch of my autobiography, I have thought that the attempt would amuse me, and might possibly interest my children or their children. I know that it would have interested me greatly to have read ever so short and dull a sketch of the mind of my grandfather, written by himself, and

[1] The late Mr. Hensleigh Wedgwood's house in Surrey.

what he thought and did, and how he worked. I have attempted to write the following account of myself, as if I were a dead man in another world looking back at my own life. Nor have I found this difficult, for life is nearly over with me. I have taken no pains about my style of writing.

I was born at Shrewsbury on February 12th, 1809, and my earliest recollection goes back only to when I was a few months over four years old, when we went to near Abergele for sea-bathing, and I recollect some events and places there with some little distinctness.

My mother died in July 1817, when I was a little over eight years old, and it is odd that I can remember hardly anything about her except her deathbed, her black velvet gown, and her curiously constructed work-table. In the spring of this same year I was sent to a day-school in Shrewsbury, where I stayed a year. I have been told that I was much slower in learning than my younger sister Catherine, and I believe that I was in many ways a naughty boy.

By the time I went to this day-school [1] my taste for natural history, and more especially for collecting, was well developed. I tried to make out the names of plants, and collected all sorts of things, shells,

[1] Kept by Rev. G. Case, minister of the Unitarian Chapel in the High Street. Mrs. Darwin was a Unitarian and attended Mr. Case's chapel, and my father as a little boy went there with his elder sisters. But both he and his brother were christened and intended to belong to the Church of England ; and after his early boyhood he seems usually to have gone to church and not to Mr. Case's. It appears (*St. James's Gazette*, December 15, 1883) that a mural tablet has been erected to his memory in the chapel, which is now known as the " Free Christian Church."—F. D.

seals, franks, coins, and minerals. The passion for collecting which leads a man to be a systematic naturalist, a virtuoso, or a miser, was very strong in me, and was clearly innate, as none of my sisters or brother ever had this taste.

One little event during this year has fixed itself very firmly in my mind, and I hope that it has done so from my conscience having been afterwards sorely troubled by it ; it is curious as showing that apparently I was interested at this early age in the variability of plants ! I told another little boy (I believe it was Leighton,[1] who afterwards became a well-known lichenologist and botanist) that I could produce variously coloured polyanthuses and primroses by watering them with certain coloured fluids, which was of course a monstrous fable, and had never been tried by me. I may here also confess that as a little boy I was much given to inventing deliberate falsehoods, and this was always done for the sake of causing excitement. For instance, I once gathered much valuable fruit from my father's trees and hid it in the shrubbery, and then ran in breathless haste to spread the news that I had discovered a hoard of stolen fruit.[2]

[1] Rev. W. A. Leighton remembers his bringing a flower to school and saying that his mother had taught him how by looking at the inside of the blossom the name of the plant could be discovered. Mr. Leighton goes on, " This greatly roused my attention and curiosity, and I inquired of him repeatedly how this could be done ? "—but his lesson was naturally enough not transmissible.—F. D.

[2] His father wisely treated this tendency not by making crimes of the fibs, but by making light of the discoveries.—F. D.

I must have been a very simple little fellow when I first went to the school. A boy of the name of Garnett took me into a cake-shop one day, and bought some cakes for which he did not pay, as the shopman trusted him. When we came out I asked him why he did not pay for them, and he instantly answered, " Why, do you not know that my uncle left a great sum of money to the town on condition that every tradesman should give whatever was wanted without payment to any one who wore his old hat and moved [it] in a particular manner ? " and he then showed me how it was moved. He then went into another shop where he was trusted, and asked for some small article, moving his hat in the proper manner, and of course obtained it without payment. When we came out he said, " Now if you like to go by yourself into that cake-shop (how well I remember its exact position), I will lend you my hat, and you can get whatever you like if you move the hat on your head properly." I gladly accepted the generous offer, and went in and asked for some cakes, moved the old hat, and was walking out of the shop, when the shopman made a rush at me, so I dropped the cakes and ran for dear life, and was astonished by being greeted with shouts of laughter by my false friend Garnett.

I can say in my own favour that I was as a boy humane, but I owed this entirely to the instruction and example of my sisters. I doubt indeed whether humanity is a natural or innate quality. I was very fond of collecting eggs, but I never took more than a single egg out of a bird's nest, except on one single occasion, when I took all, not for their value, but from a sort of bravado.

4

I had a strong taste for angling, and would sit for any number of hours on the bank of a river or pond watching the float ; when at Maer [1] I was told that I could kill the worms with salt and water, and from that day I never spitted a living worm, though at the expense probably of some loss of success.

Once as a very little boy whilst at the day-school, or before that time, I acted cruelly, for I beat a puppy, I believe, simply from enjoying the sense of power ; but the beating could not have been severe, for the puppy did not howl, of which I feel sure as the spot was near the house. This act lay heavily on my conscience, as is shown by my remembering the exact spot where the crime was committed. It probably lay all the heavier from my love of dogs being then, and for a long time afterwards, a passion. Dogs seemed to know this, for I was an adept in robbing their love from their masters.

I remember clearly only one other incident during this year whilst at Mr. Case's daily school,—namely, the burial of a dragoon soldier ; and it is surprising how clearly I can still see the horse with the man's empty boots and carbine suspended to the saddle, and the firing over the grave. This scene deeply stirred whatever poetic fancy there was in me. [2]

---

[1] The house of his uncle, Josiah Wedgwood, the younger.

[2] It is curious that another Shrewsbury boy should have been impressed by this military funeral ; Mr. Gretton, in his *Memory's Harkback*, says that the scene is so strongly impressed on his mind that he could " walk straight to the spot in St. Chad's churchyard where the poor fellow was buried." The soldier was an Inniskilling Dragoon, and the officer in command had been recently wounded at Waterloo, where his corps did good service against the French Cuirassiers.

In the summer of 1818 I went to Dr. Butler's great school in Shrewsbury, and remained there for seven years till Midsummer 1825, when I was sixteen years old. I boarded at this school, so that I had the great advantage of living the life of a true school-boy ; but as the distance was hardly more than a mile to my home, I very often ran there in the longer intervals between the callings over and before locking up at night. This, I think, was in many ways advantageous to me by keeping up home affections and interests. I remember in the early part of my school life that I often had to run very quickly to be in time, and from being a fleet runner was generally successful ; but when in doubt I prayed earnestly to God to help me, and I well remember that I attributed my success to the prayers and not to my quick running, and marvelled how generally I was aided.

I have heard my father and elder sister say that I had, as a very young boy, a strong taste for long solitary walks ; but what I thought about I know not. I often became quite absorbed, and once, whilst returning to school on the summit of the old fortifications round Shrewsbury, which had been converted into a public foot-path with no parapet on one side, I walked off and fell to the ground, but the height was only seven or eight feet. Nevertheless, the number of thoughts which passed through my mind during this very short, but sudden and wholly unexpected fall, was astonishing, and seem hardly compatible with what physiologists have, I believe, proved about each thought requiring quite an appreciable amount of time.

Nothing could have been worse for the development of my mind than Dr. Butler's school, as it was strictly classical, nothing else being taught, except a little ancient geography and history. The school as a means of education to me was simply a blank. During my whole life I have been singularly incapable of mastering any language. Especial attention was paid to verse-making, and this I could never do well. I had many friends, and got together a good collection of old verses, which by patching together, sometimes aided by other boys, I could work into any subject. Much attention was paid to learning by heart the lessons of the previous day ; this I could effect with great facility, learning forty or fifty lines of Virgil or Homer, whilst I was in morning chapel ; but this exercise was utterly useless, for every verse was forgotten in forty-eight hours. I was not idle, and with the exception of versification, generally worked conscientiously at my classics, not using cribs. The sole pleasure I ever received from such studies, was from some of the odes of Horace, which I admired greatly.

When I left the school I was for my age neither high nor low in it ; and I believe that I was considered by all my masters and by my father as a very ordinary boy, rather below the common standard in intellect. To my deep mortification my father once said to me, " You care for nothing but shooting, dogs, and rat-catching, and you will be a disgrace to yourself and all your family." But my father, who was the kindest man I ever knew, and whose memory I love with all my heart, must have been angry and somewhat unjust when he used such words.

Looking back as well as I can at my character during my school life, the only qualities which at this period promised well for the future, were, that I had strong and diversified tastes, much zeal for whatever interested me, and a keen pleasure in understanding any complex subject or thing. I was taught Euclid by a private tutor, and I distinctly remember the intense satisfaction which the clear geometrical proofs gave me. I remember with equal distinctness the delight which my uncle gave me (the father of Francis Galton) by explaining the principle of the vernier of a barometer. With respect to diversified tastes, independently of science, I was fond of reading various books, and I used to sit for hours reading the historical plays of Shakespeare, generally in an old window in the thick walls of the school. I read also other poetry, such as Thomson's *Seasons*, and the recently published poems of Byron and Scott. I mention this because later in life I wholly lost, to my great regret, all pleasure from poetry of any· kind, including Shakespeare. In connection with pleasure from poetry, I may add that in 1822 a vivid delight in scenery was first awakened in my mind, during a riding tour on the borders of Wales, and this has lasted longer than any other æsthetic pleasure.

Early in my school-days a boy had a copy of the *Wonders of the World*, which I often read, and disputed with other boys about the veracity of some of the statements ; and I believe that this book first gave me a wish to travel in remote countries, which was ultimately fulfilled by the voyage of the *Beagle*. In the latter part of my school life I became passion-

8

ately fond of shooting ; I do not believe that any one could have shown more zeal for the most holy cause than I did for shooting birds. How well I remember killing my first snipe, and my excitement was so great that I had much difficulty in reloading my gun from the trembling of my hands. This taste long continued, and I became a very good shot. When at Cambridge I used to practise throwing up my gun to my shoulder before a looking-glass to see that I threw it up straight. Another and better plan was to get a friend to wave about a lighted candle, and then to fire at it with a cap on the nipple, and if the aim was accurate the little puff of air would blow out the candle. The explosion of the cap caused a sharp crack, and I was told that the tutor of the college remarked, " What an extraordinary thing it is, Mr. Darwin seems to spend hours in cracking a horse-whip in his room, for I often hear the crack when I pass under his windows."

I had many friends amongst the schoolboys, whom I loved dearly, and I think that my disposition was then very affectionate.

With respect to science, I continued collecting minerals with much zeal, but quite unscientifically —all that I cared about was a new-named mineral, and I hardly attempted to classify them. I must have observed insects with some little care, for when ten years old (1819) I went for three weeks to Plas Edwards on the sea-coast in Wales, I was very much interested and surprised at seeing a large black and scarlet Hemipterous insect, many moths (Zygœna) and a Cicindela, which are not found in Shropshire. I almost made up my mind to begin collecting all the insects which I could find dead, for on consulting my sister, I concluded that it was not right to kill insects for the sake of making a collection. From reading White's *Selborne*, I took much pleasure in watching the habits of birds, and even made notes on the subject. In my simplicity, I remember wondering why every gentleman did not become an ornithologist.

Towards the close of my school life, my brother worked hard at chemistry, and made a fair laboratory with proper apparatus in the tool-house in the garden, and I was allowed to aid him as a servant in most of his experiments. He made all the gases and many compounds, and I read with care several books on chemistry, such as Henry and Parkes' *Chemical Catechism*. The subject interested me greatly, and we often used to go on working till rather late at night. This was the best part of my education at school, for it showed me practically the meaning of experimental science. The fact that we worked at chemistry somehow got known at school, and as it was an unprecedented fact, I was nicknamed " Gas." I was also once publicly rebuked by the head-master, Dr. Butler, for thus wasting my time on such useless subjects ; and he called me very unjustly a " poco curante," and as I did not understand what he meant, it seemed to me a fearful reproach.

As I was doing no good at school, my father wisely took me away at a rather earlier age than usual, and sent me (October 1825) to Edinburgh [1] Univer-

---

[1] He lodged at Mrs. Mackay's, 11, Lothian Street. What little the records of Edinburgh University can reveal has been published in the *Edinburgh Weekly Dispatch*, May 22, 1888 ; and in the *St. James's Gazette*, February 16, 1888. From the

sity with my brother, where I stayed for two years or sessions. My brother was completing his medical studies, though I do not believe he ever really intended to practise, and I was sent there to commence them. But soon after this period I became convinced from various small circumstances that my father would leave me property enough to subsist on with some comfort, though I never imagined that I should be so rich a man as I am ; but my belief was sufficient to check any strenuous effort to learn medicine.

The instruction at Edinburgh was altogether by lectures, and these were intolerably dull, with the exception of those on chemistry by Hope ; but to my mind there are no advantages and many disadvantages in lectures compared with reading. Dr. Duncan's lectures on Materia Medica at 8 o'clock on a winter's morning are something fearful to remember. Dr. Munro made his lectures on human anatomy as dull as he was himself, and the subject disgusted me. It has proved one of the greatest evils in my life that I was not urged to practise dissection, for I should soon have got over my disgust, and the practice would have been invaluable for all my future work. This has been an irremediable evil, as well as my incapacity to draw. I also attended regularly the clinical wards in the hospital. Some of the cases distressed me a good deal, and I still have vivid pictures before me of some of them ; but I was not so foolish as to allow this to lessen my attendance. I cannot understand why this part of my medical

latter journal it appears that he and his brother Erasmus made more use of the library than was usual among the students of their time.

course did not interest me in a greater degree ; for during the summer before coming to Edinburgh, I began attending some of the poor people, chiefly children and women in Shrewsbury : I wrote down as full an account as I could of the case with all the symptoms, and read them aloud to my father, who suggested further enquiries and advised me what medicines to give, which I made up myself. At one time I had at least a dozen patients, and I felt a keen interest in the work.[1] My father, who was by far the best judge of character whom I ever knew, declared that I should make a successful physician,—meaning by this, one who would get many patients. He maintained that the chief element of success was exciting confidence ; but what he saw in me which convinced him that I should create confidence I know not. I also attended on two occasions the operating theatre in the hospital at Edinburgh, and saw two very bad operations, one on a child, but I rushed away before they were completed. Nor did I ever attend again, for hardly any inducement would have been strong enough to make me do so ; this being long before the blessed days of chloroform. The two cases fairly haunted me for many a long year.

My brother stayed only one year at the University, so that during the second year I was left to my own resources ; and this was an advantage, for I became well acquainted with several young men fond of natural science. One of these was Ainsworth, who

[1] I have heard him call to mind the pride he felt at the results of the successful treatment of a whole family with tartar emetic.—F. D.

afterwards published his travels in Assyria ; he was a Wernerian geologist, and knew a little about many subjects. Dr. Coldstream [1] was a very different young man, prim, formal, highly religious, and most kind-hearted ; he afterwards published some good zoological articles. A third young man was Hardie, who would, I think, have made a good botanist, but died early in India. Lastly, Dr. Grant, my senior by several years, but how I became acquainted with him I cannot remember ; he published some first-rate zoological papers, but after coming to London as Professor in University College, he did nothing more in science, a fact which has always been inexplicable to me. I knew him well ; he was dry and formal in manner, with much enthusiasm beneath this outer crust. He one day, when we were walking together, burst forth in high admiration of Lamarck and his views on evolution. I listened in silent astonishment, and as far as I can judge, without any effect on my mind. I had previously read the *Zoonomia* of my grandfather, in which similar views are maintained, but without producing any effect on me. Nevertheless it is probable that the hearing rather early in life such views maintained and praised may have favoured my upholding them under a different form in my *Origin of Species*. At this time I admired greatly the *Zoonomia* ; but on reading it a second time after an interval of ten or fifteen years, I was much disappointed ; the proportion of speculation being so large to the facts given.

[1] Dr. Coldstream died September 17, 1863 ; see Crown 16mo. Book Tract, No. 19, of the Religious Tract Society (no date).

Drs. Grant and Coldstream attended much to marine Zoology, and I often accompanied the former to collect animals in the tidal pools, which I dissected as well as I could. I also became friends with some of the Newhaven fishermen, and sometimes accompanied them when they trawled for oysters, and thus got many specimens. But from not having had any regular practice in dissection, and from possessing only a wretched microscope, my attempts were very poor. Nevertheless I made one interesting little discovery, and read, about the beginning of the year 1826, a short paper on the subject before the Plinian Society. This was that the so-called ova of Flustra had the power of independent movement by means of cilia, and were in fact larvæ. In another short paper, I showed that the little globular bodies which had been supposed to be the young state of *Fucus loreus* were the egg-cases of the worm-like *Pontobdella muricata*.

The Plinian Society [1] was encouraged and, I believe, founded by Professor Jameson : it consisted of students, and met in an underground room in the University for the sake of reading papers on natural science and discussing them. I used regularly to attend, and the meetings had a good effect on me in stimulating my zeal and giving me new congenial acquaintances. One evening a poor young man got up, and after stammering for a prodigious length of time, blushing crimson, he at last slowly got out the words, " Mr. President, I have forgotten what I was going to say." The poor fellow looked quite over-

[1] The society was founded in 1823, and expired about 1848 (*Edinburgh Weekly Dispatch*, May 22, 1888).

whelmed, and all the members were so surprised that no one could think of a word to say to cover his confusion. The papers which were read to our little society were not printed, so that I had not the satisfaction of seeing my paper in print ; but I believe Dr. Grant noticed my small discovery in his excellent memoir on Flustra.

I was also a member of the Royal Medical Society, and attended pretty regularly ; but as the subjects were exclusively medical, I did not much care about them. Much rubbish was talked there, but there were some good speakers, of whom the best was the [late] Sir J. Kay-Shuttleworth. Dr. Grant took me occasionally to the meetings of the Wernerian Society, where various papers on natural history were read, discussed, and afterwards published in the Transactions. I heard Audubon deliver there some interesting discourses on the habits of N. American birds, sneering somewhat unjustly at Waterton. By the way, a negro lived in Edinburgh, who had travelled with Waterton, and gained his livelihood by stuffing birds, which he did excellently ; he gave me lessons for payment, and I used often to sit with him, for he was a very pleasant and intelligent man.

Mr. Leonard Horner also took me once to a meeting of the Royal Society of Edinburgh, where I saw Sir Walter Scott in the chair as President, and he apologised to the meeting as not feeling fitted for such a position. I looked at him and at the whole scene with some awe and reverence, and I think it was owing to this visit during my youth, and to my having attended the Royal Medical Society, that I felt the honour of being elected a few years ago an honorary

member of both these Societies, more than any other
similar honour. If I had been told at that time that I
should one day have been thus honoured, I declare
that I should have thought it as ridiculous and improbable as if I had been told that I should be elected
King of England.

During my second year at Edinburgh I attended
Jameson's lectures on Geology and Zoology, but they
were incredibly dull. The sole effect they produced
on me was the determination never as long as I
lived to read a book on Geology, or in any way to
study the science. Yet I feel sure that I was prepared
for a philosophical treatment of the subject ; for an
old Mr. Cotton, in Shropshire, who knew a good deal
about rocks, had pointed out to me two or three
years previously a well-known large erratic boulder
in the town of Shrewsbury, called the " bell-stone " ;
he told me that there was no rock of the same kind
nearer than Cumberland or Scotland, and he solemnly
assured me that the world would come to an end
before any one would be able to explain how this
stone came where it now lay. This produced a deep
impression on me, and I meditated over this wonderful
stone. So that I felt the keenest delight when I
first read of the action of icebergs in transporting
boulders, and I gloried in the progress of Geology.
Equally striking is the fact that I, though now only
sixty-seven years old, heard the Professor, in a field
lecture at Salisbury Craigs, discoursing on a trap-
dyke, with amygdaloidal margins and the strata
indurated on each side, with volcanic rocks all around
us, say that it was a fissure filled with sediment from
above, adding with a sneer that there were men who

maintained that it had been injected from beneath in a molten condition. When I think of this lecture, I do not wonder that I determined never to attend to Geology.

From attending Jameson's lectures, I became acquainted with the curator of the museum, Mr. Macgillivray, who afterwards published a large and excellent book on the birds of Scotland. I had much interesting natural-history talk with him, and he was very kind to me. He gave me some rare shells, for I at that time collected marine mollusca, but with no great zeal.

My summer vacations during these two years were wholly given up to amusements, though I always had some book in hand, which I read with interest. During the summer of 1826, I took a long walking tour with two friends with knapsacks on our backs through North Wales. We walked thirty miles most days, including one day the ascent of Snowdon. I also went with my sister a riding tour in North Wales, a servant with saddle-bags carrying our clothes. The autumns were devoted to shooting, chiefly at Mr. Owen's, at Woodhouse, and at my Uncle Jos's,[1] at Maer. My zeal was so great that I used to place my shooting-boots open by my bed-side when I went to bed, so as not to lose half a minute in putting them on in the morning ; and on one occasion I reached a distant part of the Maer estate, on the 20th of August for black-game shooting, before I could see : I then toiled on with the gamekeeper the whole day through thick heath and young Scotch firs.

[1] Josiah Wedgwood, the son of the founder of the Etruria Works.

I kept an exact record of every bird which I shot throughout the whole season. One day when shooting at Woodhouse with Captain Owen, the eldest son, and Major Hill, his cousin, afterwards Lord Berwick, both of whom I liked very much, I thought myself shamefully used, for every time after I had fired and thought that I had killed a bird, one of the two acted as if loading his gun, and cried out, " You must not count that bird, for I fired at the same time," and the gamekeeper, perceiving the joke, backed them up. After some hours they told me the joke, but it was no joke to me, for I had shot a large number of birds, but did not know how many, and could not add them to my list, which I used to do by making a knot in a piece of string tied to a button-hole. This my wicked friends had perceived.

How I did enjoy shooting ! but I think that I must have been half-consciously ashamed of my zeal, for I tried to persuade myself that shooting was almost an intellectual employment ; it required so much skill to judge where to find most game and to hunt the dogs well.

One of my autumnal visits to Maer in 1827 was memorable from meeting there Sir J. Mackintosh, who was the best converser I ever listened to. I heard afterwards with a glow of pride that he had said, " There is something in that young man that interests me." This must have been chiefly due to his perceiving that I listened with much interest to everything which he said, for I was as ignorant as a pig about his subjects of history, politics, and moral philosophy. To hear of praise from an eminent person, though no doubt apt or certain to excite vanity, is, I think, good for a young man, as it helps to keep him in the right course.

My visits to Maer during these two or three succeeding years were quite delightful, independently of the autumnal shooting. Life there was perfectly free ; the country was very pleasant for walking or riding ; and in the evening there was much very agreeable conversation, not so personal as it generally is in large family parties, together with music. In the summer the whole family used often to sit on the steps of the old portico with the flower-garden in front, and with the steep wooded bank opposite the house reflected in the lake, with here and there a fish rising or a water-bird paddling about. Nothing has left a more vivid picture on my mind than these evenings at Maer. I was also attached to and greatly revered my Uncle Jos ; he was silent and reserved, so as to be a rather awful man ; but he sometimes talked openly with me. He was the very type of an upright man, with the clearest judgment. I do not believe that any power on earth could have made him swerve an inch from what he considered the right course. I used to apply to him in my mind the well-known ode of Horace, now forgotten by me, in which the words " nec vultus tyranni, &c.," [1] come in.

Cambridge, 1828–1831.—After having spent two sessions in Edinburgh, my father perceived, or he heard from my sisters, that I did not like the thought

[1] Justum et tenacem propositi virum
Non civium ardor prava jubentium,
Non vultus instantis tyranni
Mente quatit solidâ.

of being a physician, so he proposed that I should
become a clergyman. He was very properly vehe-
ment against my turning into an idle sporting man,
which then seemed my probable destination. I asked
for some time to consider, as from what little I had
heard or thought on the subject I had scruples about
declaring my belief in all the dogmas of the Church
of England ; though otherwise I liked the thought
of being a country clergyman. Accordingly I read
with great care *Pearson on the Creed,* and a few other
books on divinity ; and as I did not then in the least
doubt the strict and literal truth of every word in
the Bible, I soon persuaded myself that our Creed
must be fully accepted.

Considering how fiercely I have been attacked by
the orthodox, it seems ludicrous that I once intended
to be a clergyman. Nor was this intention and
my father's wish ever formally given up, but died a
natural death when, on leaving Cambridge, I joined
the *Beagle* as naturalist. If the phrenologists are to
be trusted, I was well fitted in one respect to be a
clergyman. A few years ago the secretaries of a
German psychological society asked me earnestly by
letter for a photograph of myself ; and some time
afterwards I received the proceedings of one of the
meetings, in which it seemed that the shape of my
head had been the subject of a public discussion, and
one of the speakers declared that I had the bump of
reverence developed enough for ten priests.

As it was decided that I should be a clergyman, it
was necessary that I should go to one of the English
universities and take a degree ; but as I had never
opened a classical book since leaving school, I found

to my dismay that, in the two intervening years, I had actually forgotten, incredible as it may appear, almost everything which I had learnt, even to some few of the Greek letters. I did not therefore proceed to Cambridge at the usual time in October, but worked with a private tutor in Shrewsbury, and went to Cambridge after the Christmas vacation, early in 1828. I soon recovered my school standard of knowledge, and could translate easy Greek books, such as Homer and the Greek Testament, with moderate facility.

During the three years which I spent at Cambridge my time was wasted, as far as the academical studies were concerned, as completely as at Edinburgh and at school. I attempted mathematics, and even went during the summer of 1828 with a private tutor to Barmouth, but I got on very slowly. The work was repugnant to me, chiefly from my not being able to see any meaning in the early steps in algebra. This impatience was very foolish, and in after years I have deeply regretted that I did not proceed far enough at least to understand something of the great leading principles of mathematics, for men thus endowed seem to have an extra sense. But I do not believe that I should ever have succeeded beyond a very low grade. With respect to Classics I did nothing except attend a few compulsory college lectures, and the attendance was almost nominal. In my second year I had to work for a month or two to pass the Little-Go, which I did easily. Again, in my last year I worked with some earnestness for my final degree of B.A., and brushed up my Classics, together with a little Algebra and Euclid, which latter gave me much pleasure, as it did at school. In order to pass the B.A. examination, it was also necessary to get up Paley's *Evidences of Christianity*, and his *Moral Philosophy*. This was done in a thorough manner, and I am convinced that I could have written out the whole of the *Evidences* with perfect correctness, but not of course in the clear language of Paley. The logic of this book and, as I may add, of his *Natural Theology*, gave me as much delight as did Euclid. The careful study of these works, without attempting to learn any part by rote, was the only part of the academical course which, as I then felt, and as I still believe, was of the least use to me in the education of my mind. I did not at that time trouble myself about Paley's premises ; and taking these on trust, I was charmed and convinced by the long line of argumentation. By answering well the examination questions in Paley, by doing Euclid well, and by not failing miserably in Classics, I gained a good place among the οἱ πολλοί or crowd of men who do not go in for honours. Oddly enough, I cannot remember how high I stood, and my memory fluctuates between the fifth, tenth, or twelfth name on the list.[1]

Public lectures on several branches were given in the University, attendance being quite voluntary ; but I was so sickened with lectures at Edinburgh that I did not even attend Sedgwick's eloquent and interesting lectures. Had I done so I should probably have become a geologist earlier than I did. I attended, however, Henslow's lectures on Botany, and liked them much for their extreme clearness, and the admir-

[1] Tenth in the list of January 1831.

able illustrations; but I did not study botany. Henslow used to take his pupils, including several of the older members of the University, field excursions, on foot or in coaches, to distant places, or in a barge down the river, and lectured on the rarer plants and animals which were observed. These excursions were delightful.

Although, as we shall presently see, there were some redeeming features in my life at Cambridge, my time was sadly wasted there, and worse than wasted. From my passion for shooting and for hunting, and, when this failed, for riding across country, I got into a sporting set, including some dissipated low-minded young men. We used often to dine together in the evening, though these dinners often included men of a higher stamp, and we sometimes drank too much, with jolly singing and playing at cards afterwards. I know that I ought to feel ashamed of days and evenings thus spent, but as some of my friends were very pleasant, and we were all in the highest spirits, I cannot help looking back to these times with much pleasure.[1]

But I am glad to think that I had many other friends of a widely different nature. I was very intimate with Whitley,[2] who was afterwards Senior Wrangler, and we used continually to take long walks together. He inoculated me with a taste for pictures and good engravings, of which I bought some. I

[1] I gather from some of my father's contemporaries that he has exaggerated the Bacchanalian nature of these parties.— F. D.

[2] Rev. C. Whitley, Hon. Canon of Durham, formerly Reader in Natural Philosophy in Durham University.

frequently went to the Fitzwilliam Gallery, and my taste must have been fairly good, for I certainly admired the best pictures, which I discussed with the old curator. I read also with much interest Sir Joshua Reynolds' book. This taste, though not natural to me, lasted for several years, and many of the pictures in the National Gallery in London gave me much pleasure; that of Sebastian del Piombo exciting in me a sense of sublimity.

I also got into a musical set, I believe by means of my warm-hearted friend, Herbert,[1] who took a high wrangler's degree. From associating with these men, and hearing them play, I acquired a strong taste for music, and used very often to time my walks so as to hear on week days the anthem in King's College Chapel. This gave me intense pleasure, so that my backbone would sometimes shiver. I am sure that there was no affectation or mere imitation in this taste, for I used generally to go by myself to King's College, and I sometimes hired the chorister boys to sing in my rooms. Nevertheless I am so utterly destitute of an ear, that I cannot perceive a discord, or keep time and hum a tune correctly; and it is a mystery how I could possibly have derived pleasure from music.

My musical friends soon perceived my state, and sometimes amused themselves by making me pass an examination, which consisted in ascertaining how many tunes I could recognise, when they were played rather more quickly or slowly than usual. ' God save the King,' when thus played, was a sore puzzle.

[1] The late John Maurice Herbert, County Court Judge of Cardiff and the Monmouth Circuit.

There was another man with almost as bad an ear as I had, and strange to say he played a little on the flute. Once I had the triumph of beating him in one of our musical examinations.

But no pursuit at Cambridge was followed with nearly so much eagerness or gave me so much pleasure as collecting beetles. It was the mere passion for collecting, for I did not dissect them, and rarely compared their external characters with published descriptions, but got them named anyhow. I will give a proof of my zeal : one day, on tearing off some old bark, I saw two rare beetles, and seized one in each hand ; then I saw a third and new kind, which I could not bear to lose, so that I popped the one which I held in my right hand into my mouth. Alas ! it ejected some intensely acrid fluid, which burnt my tongue so that I was forced to spit the beetle out, which was lost, as was the third one.

I was very successful in collecting, and invented two new methods ; I employed a labourer to scrape, during the winter, moss off old trees and place it in a large bag, and likewise to collect the rubbish at the bottom of the barges in which reeds are brought from the fens, and thus I got some very rare species. No poet ever felt more delighted at seeing his first poem published than I did at seeing, in Stephen's *Illustrations of British Insects*, the magic words, " captured by C. Darwin, Esq." I was introduced to entomology by my second cousin, W. Darwin Fox, a clever and most pleasant man, who was then at Christ's College, and with whom I became extremely intimate. Afterwards I became well acquainted, and went out collecting, with Albert Way of Trinity, who in after years became a well-known archæologist ; also with H. Thompson,[1] of the same College, afterwards a leading agriculturist, chairman of a great railway, and Member of Parliament. It seems, therefore, that a taste for collecting beetles is some indication of future success in life.

I am surprised what an indelible impression many of the beetles which I caught at Cambridge have left on my mind. I can remember the exact appearance of certain posts, old trees and banks where I made a good capture. The pretty *Panagæus crux-major* was a treasure in those days, and here at Down I saw a beetle running across a walk, and on picking it up instantly perceived that it differed slightly from *P. crux-major*, and it turned out to be *P. quadripunctatus*, which is only a variety or closely allied species, differing from it very slightly in outline. I had never seen in those old days Licinus alive, which to an uneducated eye hardly differs from many of the black Carabidous beetles ; but my sons found here a specimen, and I instantly recognised that it was new to me ; yet I had not looked at a British beetle for the last twenty years.

I have not yet mentioned a circumstance which influenced my whole career more than any other. This was my friendship with Professor Henslow. Before coming up to Cambridge, I had heard of him from my brother as a man who knew every branch of science, and I was accordingly prepared to reverence him. He kept open house once every week [2]

[1] Afterwards Sir H. Thompson, first baronet.
[2] The *Cambridge Ray Club*, which in 1887 attained its fiftieth anniversary, is the direct descendant of these meetings,

when all undergraduates and some older members of the University, who were attached to science, used to meet in the evening. I soon got, through Fox, an invitation, and went there regularly. Before long I became well acquainted with Henslow, and during the latter half of my time at Cambridge took long walks with him on most days ; so that I was called by some of the dons " the man who walks with Henslow " ; and in the evening I was very often asked to join his family dinner. His knowledge was great in botany, entomology, chemistry, mineralogy, and geology. His strongest taste was to draw conclusions from long-continued minute observations. His judgment was excellent, and his whole mind well-balanced ; but I do not suppose that any one would say that he possessed much original genius.

He was deeply religious, and so orthodox, that he told me one day he should be grieved if a single word of the Thirty-nine Articles were altered. His moral qualities were in every way admirable. He was free from every tinge of vanity or other petty feeling ; and I never saw a man who thought so little about himself or his own concerns. His temper was imperturbably good, with the most winning and courteous manners ; yet, as I have seen, he could be roused by any bad action to the warmest indignation and prompt action.

I once saw in his company in the streets of Cambridge almost as horrid a scene as could have been witnessed during the French Revolution. Two body--

having been founded to fill the blank caused by the discontinuance, in 1836, of Henslow's Friday evenings. See Professor Babington's pamphlet, *The Cambridge Ray Club*, 1887.

snatchers had been arrested, and whilst being taken
to prison had been torn from the constable by a
crowd of the roughest men, who dragged them by
their legs along the muddy and stony road. They
were covered from head to foot with mud, and their
faces were bleeding either from having been kicked
or from the stones ; they looked like corpses, but the
crowd was so dense that I got only a few momentary
glimpses of the wretched creatures. Never in my
life have I seen such wrath painted on a man's face
as was shown by Henslow at this horrid scene. He
tried repeatedly to penetrate the mob ; but it was
simply impossible. He then rushed away to the
mayor, telling me not to follow him, but to get more
policemen. I forget the issue, except that the two
men were got into the prison without being killed.

Henslow's benevolence was unbounded, as he
proved by his many excellent schemes for his poor
parishioners, when in after years he held the living
of Hitcham. My intimacy with such a man ought to
have been, and I hope was, an inestimable benefit.
I cannot resist mentioning a trifling incident, which
showed his kind consideration. Whilst examining
some pollen-grains on a damp surface, I saw the
tubes exserted, and instantly rushed off to communicate my surprising discovery to him. Now I do
not suppose any other professor of botany could
have helped laughing at my coming in such a hurry
to make such a communication. But he agreed how
interesting the phenomenon was, and explained its
meaning, but made me clearly understand how well
it was known ; so I left him not in the least mortified,
but well pleased at having discovered for myself

so remarkable a fact, but determined not to be in such a hurry again to communicate my discoveries.

Dr. Whewell was one of the older and distinguished men who sometimes visited Henslow, and on several occasions I walked home with him at night. Next to Sir J. Mackintosh he was the best converser on grave subjects to whom I ever listened. Leonard Jenyns,[1] who afterwards published some good essays in Natural History, often stayed with Henslow, who was his brother-in-law. I visited him at his parsonage on the borders of the Fens [Swaffham Bulbeck], and had many a good walk and talk with him about Natural History. I became also acquainted with several other men older than me, who did not care much about science, but were friends of Henslow. One was a Scotchman, brother of Sir Alexander Ramsay, and tutor of Jesus College ; he was a delightful man, but did not live for many years. Another was Mr. Dawes, afterwards Dean of Hereford, and famous for his success in the education of the poor. These men and others of the same standing, together with Henslow, used sometimes to take distant excursions into the country, which I was allowed to join, and they were most agreeable.

Looking back, I infer that there must have been something in me a little superior to the common run of youths, otherwise the above-mentioned men, so

[1] Mr. Jenyns (now Blomefield) described the fish for the *Zoology of the Voyage of H.M.S. Beagle* ; and is author of a long series of papers, chiefly zoological. In 1887 he printed, for private circulation, an autobiographical sketch, *Chapters in my Life*, and subsequently some (undated) addenda. The well-known Soame Jenyns was cousin to Mr. Jenyns' father.

much older than me and higher in academical position, would never have allowed me to associate with them. Certainly I was not aware of any such superiority, and I remember one of my sporting friends, Turner, who saw me at work with my beetles, saying that I should some day be a Fellow of the Royal Society, and the notion seemed to me preposterous.

During my last year at Cambridge, I read with care and profound interest Humboldt's *Personal Narrative*. This work, and Sir J. Herschel's *Introduction to the Study of Natural Philosophy*, stirred up in me a burning zeal to add even the most humble contribution to the noble structure of Natural Science. No one or a dozen other books influenced me nearly so much as these two. I copied out from Humboldt long passages about Teneriffe, and read them aloud on one of the above-mentioned excursions, to (I think) Henslow, Ramsay, and Dawes, for on a previous occasion I had talked about the glories of Teneriffe, and some of the party declared they would endeavour to go there ; but I think they were only half in earnest. I was, however, quite in earnest, and got an introduction to a merchant in London to enquire about ships ; but the scheme was, of course, knocked on the head by the voyage of the *Beagle*.

My summer vacations were given up to collecting beetles, to some reading, and short tours. In the autumn my whole time was devoted to shooting, chiefly at Woodhouse and Maer, and sometimes with young Eyton of Eyton. Upon the whole the three years which I spent at Cambridge were the most joyful in my happy life ; for I was then in excellent health, and almost always in high spirits.

As I had at first come up to Cambridge at Christmas, I was forced to keep two terms after passing my final examination, at the commencement of 1831 ; and Henslow then persuaded me to begin the study of geology. Therefore on my return to Shropshire I examined sections, and coloured a map of parts round Shrewsbury. Professor Sedgwick intended to visit North Wales in the beginning of August to pursue his famous geological investigations amongst the older rocks, and Henslow asked him to allow me to accompany him.[1] Accordingly he came and slept at my father's house.

A short conversation with him during this evening produced a strong impression on my mind. Whilst examining an old gravel-pit near Shrewsbury, a labourer told me that he had found in it a large worn tropical Volute shell, such as may be seen on chimney-pieces of cottages ; and as he would not sell the shell, I was convinced that he had really found it in the pit. I told Sedgwick of the fact, and he at once said (no doubt truly) that it must have been thrown away by some one into the pit ; but then added, if really embedded there it would be the greatest misfortune to geology, as it would overthrow all that we know about the superficial deposits of the Midland Counties.

[1] In connection with this tour my father used to tell a story about Sedgwick : they had started from their inn one morning, and had walked a mile or two, when Sedgwick suddenly stopped, and vowed that he would return, being certain " that damned scoundrel " (the waiter) had not given the chambermaid the sixpence entrusted to him for the purpose. He was ultimately persuaded to give up the project, seeing that there was no reason for suspecting the waiter of perfidy. —F. D.

These gravel-beds belong in fact to the glacial period, and in after years I found in them broken arctic shells. But I was then utterly astonished at Sedgwick not being delighted at so wonderful a fact as a tropical shell being found near the surface in the middle of England. Nothing before had ever made me thoroughly realise, though I had read various scientific books, that science consists in grouping facts so that general laws or conclusions may be drawn from them.

Next morning we started for Llangollen, Conway, Bangor, and Capel Curig. This tour was of decided use in teaching me a little how to make out the geology of a country. Sedgwick often sent me on a line parallel to his, telling me to bring back specimens of the rocks and to mark the stratification on a map. I have little doubt that he did this for my good, as I was too ignorant to have aided him. On this tour I had a striking instance how easy it is to overlook phenomena, however conspicuous, before they have been observed by any one. We spent many hours in Cwm Idwal, examining all the rocks with extreme care, as Sedgwick was anxious to find fossils in them ; but neither of us saw a trace of the wonderful glacial phenomena all around us ; we did not notice the plainly scored rocks, the perched boulders, the lateral and terminal moraines. Yet these phenomena are so conspicuous that, as I declared in a paper published many years afterwards in the *Philosophical Magazine*,[1] a house burnt down by fire did not tell its story more plainly than did this valley. If it had still been filled by a glacier, the phenomena would have been less distinct than they now are.

[1] *Philosophical Magazine*, 1842.

At Capel Curig I left Sedgwick and went in a straight line by compass and map across the mountains to Barmouth, never following any track unless it coincided with my course. I thus came on some strange wild places, and enjoyed much this manner of travelling. I visited Barmouth to see some Cambridge friends who were reading there, and thence returned to Shrewsbury and to Maer for shooting ; for at that time I should have thought myself mad to give up the first days of partridge-shooting for geology or any other science.

Voyage of the ' Beagle': from December 27, 1831, to October 2, 1836.

On returning home from my short geological tour in North Wales, I found a letter from Henslow, informing me that Captain Fitz-Roy was willing to give up part of his own cabin to any young man who who would volunteer to go with him without pay as naturalist to the Voyage of the *Beagle*. I have given, as I believe, in my MS. Journal an account of all the circumstances which then occurred ; I will here only say that I was instantly eager to accept the offer, but my father strongly objected, adding the words, fortunate for me, " If you can find any man of common-sense who advises you to go I will give my consent." So I wrote that evening and refused the offer. On the next morning I went to Maer to be ready for September 1st, and whilst out shooting, my uncle [1] sent for me, offering to drive me over to Shrewsbury and talk with my father, as my uncle

_____
[1] Josiah Wedgwood.

33

thought it would be wise in me to accept the offer. My father always maintained that [my uncle] was one of the most sensible men in the world, and he at once consented in the kindest manner. I had been rather extravagant at Cambridge, and to console my father, said, " that I should be deuced clever to spend more than my allowance whilst on board the *Beagle*" ; but he answered with a smile, " But they tell me you are very clever."

Next day I started for Cambridge to see Henslow, and thence to London to see Fitz-Roy, and all was soon arranged. Afterwards, on becoming very intimate with Fitz-Roy, I heard that I had run a very narrow risk of being rejected on account of the shape of my nose ! He was an ardent disciple of Lavater, and was convinced that he could judge of a man's character by the outline of his features ; and he doubted whether any one with my nose could possess sufficient energy and determination for the voyage. But I think he was afterwards well satisfied that my nose had spoken falsely.

Fitz-Roy's character was a singular one, with very many noble features : he was devoted to his duty, generous to a fault, bold, determined, and indomitably energetic, and an ardent friend to all under his sway. He would undertake any sort of trouble to assist those whom he thought deserved assistance. He was a handsome man, strikingly like a gentleman, with highly-courteous manners, which resembled those of his maternal uncle, the famous Lord Castlereagh, as I was told by the Minister at Rio. Nevertheless he must have inherited much in his appearance from Charles II., for Dr. Wallich gave me a collection of photographs which he had made, and I was struck with the resemblance of one to Fitz-Roy; and on looking at the name, I found it Ch. E. Sobieski Stuart, Count d'Albanie,[1] a descendant of the same monarch.

Fitz-Roy's temper was a most unfortunate one. It was usually worst in the early morning, and with his eagle eye he could generally detect something amiss about the ship, and was then unsparing in his blame. He was very kind to me, but was a man very difficult to live with on the intimate terms which necessarily followed from our messing by ourselves in the same cabin. We had several quarrels; for instance, early in the voyage at Bahia, in Brazil, he defended and praised slavery, which I abominated, and told me that he had just visited a great slave-owner, who had called up many of his slaves and asked them whether they were happy, and whether they wished to be free, and all answered "No." I then asked him, perhaps with a sneer, whether he thought that the answer of slaves in the presence of their master was worth anything? This made him excessively angry, and he said that as I doubted his word we could not live any longer together. I thought that I should have been compelled to leave the ship; but as soon as the news spread, which it did quickly, as the captain sent for the first lieutenant to assuage his anger by abusing me, I was deeply gratified by receiving an invitation from all the gun-

[1] The Count d'Albanie's claim to Royal descent has been shown to be based on a myth. See the *Quarterly Review*, 1847, vol. lxxxi. p. 83; also Hayward's *Biographical and Critical Essays*, 1873, vol. ii. p. 201.

room officers to mess with them. But after a few hours Fitz-Roy showed his usual magnanimity by sending an officer to me with an apology and a request that I would continue to live with him.

His character was in several respects one of the most noble which I have ever known.

The voyage of the *Beagle* has been by far the most important event in my life, and has determined my whole career; yet it depended on so small a circumstance as my uncle offering to drive me thirty miles to Shrewsbury, which few uncles would have done, and on such a trifle as the shape of my nose. I have always felt that I owe to the voyage the first real training or education of my mind; I was led to attend closely to several branches of natural history, and thus my powers of observation were improved, though they were always fairly developed.

The investigation of the geology of all the places visited was far more important, as reasoning here comes into play. On first examining a new district, nothing can appear more hopeless than the chaos of rocks; but by recording the stratification and nature of the rocks and fossils at many points, always reasoning and predicting what will be found elsewhere, light soon begins to dawn on the district, and the structure of the whole becomes more or less intelligible. I had brought with me the first volume of Lyell's *Principles of Geology*, which I studied attentively; and the book was of the highest service to me in many ways. The very first place which I examined, namely, St. Jago, in the Cape de Verde islands, showed me clearly the wonderful superiority of Lyell's manner of treating geology, compared with that of any other author whose works I had with me or ever afterwards read.

Another of my occupations was collecting animals of all classes, briefly describing and roughly dissecting many of the marine ones ; but from not being able to draw, and from not having sufficient anatomical knowledge, a great pile of MS. which I made during the voyage has proved almost useless. I thus lost much time, with the exception of that spent in acquiring some knowledge of the Crustaceans, as this was of service when in after years I undertook a monograph of the Cirripedia.

During some part of the day I wrote my Journal, and took much pains in describing carefully and vividly all that I had seen ; and this was good practice. My Journal served also, in part, as letters to my home, and portions were sent to England whenever there was an opportunity.

The above various special studies were, however, of no importance compared with the habit of energetic industry and of concentrated attention to whatever I was engaged in, which I then acquired. Everything about which I thought or read was made to bear directly on what I had seen or was likely to see ; and this habit of mind was continued during the five years of the voyage. I feel sure that it was this training which has enabled me to do whatever I have done in science.

Looking backwards, I can now perceive how my love for science gradually preponderated over every other taste. During the first two years my old passion for shooting survived in nearly full force, and I shot myself all the birds and animals for my collection ;

but gradually I gave up my gun more and more, and finally altogether, to my servant, as shooting interfered with my work, more especially with making out the geological structure of a country. I discovered, though unconsciously and insensibly, that the pleasure of observing and reasoning was a much higher one than that of skill and sport. That my mind became developed through my pursuits during the voyage is rendered probable by a remark made by my father, who was the most acute observer whom I ever saw, of a sceptical disposition, and far from being a believer in phrenology ; for on first seeing me after the voyage, he turned round to my sisters, and exclaimed, " Why, the shape of his head is quite altered."

To return to the voyage. On September 11th (1831), I paid a flying visit with Fitz-Roy to the *Beagle* at Plymouth. Thence to Shrewsbury to wish my father and sisters a long farewell. On October 24th I took up my residence at Plymouth, and remained there until December 27th, when the *Beagle* finally left the shores of England for her circumnavigation of the world. We made two earlier attempts to sail, but were driven back each time by heavy gales. These two months at Plymouth were the most miserable which I ever spent, though I exerted myself in various ways. I was out of spirits at the thought of leaving all my family and friends for so long a time, and the weather seemed to me inexpressibly gloomy. I was also troubled with palpitation and pain about the heart, and like many a young ignorant man, especially one with a smattering of medical knowledge, was convinced that I had heart disease. I did not consult any doctor, as I fully expected to hear the verdict that I was not fit for the voyage, and I was resolved to go at all hazards.

I need not here refer to the events of the voyage —where we went and what we did—as I have given a sufficiently full account in my published Journal. The glories of the vegetation of the Tropics rise before my mind at the present time more vividly than anything else ; though the sense of sublimity, which the great deserts of Patagonia and the forest-clad mountains of Tierra del Fuego excited in me, has left an indelible impression on my mind. The sight of a naked savage in his native land is an event which can never be forgotten. Many of my excursions on horseback through wild countries, or in the boats, some of which lasted several weeks, were deeply interesting ; their discomfort and some degree of danger were at that time hardly a drawback, and none at all afterwards. I also reflect with high satisfaction on some of my scientific work, such as solving the problem of coral islands, and making out the geological structure of certain islands, for instance, St. Helena. Nor must I pass over the discovery of the singular relations of the animals and plants inhabiting the several islands of the Galapagos archipelago, and of all of them to the inhabitants of South America.

As far as I can judge of myself, I worked to the utmost during the voyage from the mere pleasure of investigation, and from my strong desire to add a few facts to the great mass of facts in Natural Science. But I was also ambitious to take a fair place among scientific men,—whether more ambitious or less so than most of my fellow-workers, I can form no opinion.

The geology of St. Jago is very striking, yet simple : a stream of lava formerly flowed over the bed of the sea, formed of triturated recent shells and corals, which it has baked into a hard white rock. Since then the whole island has been upheaved. But the line of white rock revealed to me a new and important fact, namely, that there had been afterwards subsidence round the craters, which had since been in action, and had poured forth lava. It then first dawned on me that I might perhaps write a book on the geology of the various countries visited, and this made me thrill with delight. That was a memorable hour to me, and how distinctly I can call to mind the low cliff of lava beneath which I rested, with the sun glaring hot, a few strange desert plants growing near, and with living corals in the tidal pools at my feet. Later in the voyage, Fitz-Roy asked me to read some of my Journal, and declared it would be worth publishing ; so here was a second book in prospect !

Towards the close of our voyage I received a letter whilst at Ascension, in which my sisters told me that Sedgwick had called on my father, and said that I should take a place among the leading scientific men. I could not at the time understand how he could have learnt anything of my proceedings, but I heard (I believe afterwards) that Henslow had read some of the letters which I wrote to him before the Philosophical Society of Cambridge,[1] and had printed

---

[1] Read at the meeting held November 16, 1835, and printed in a pamphlet of 31 pp. for distribution among the members of the Society.

them for private distribution. My collection of fossil bones, which had been sent to Henslow, also excited considerable attention amongst palæontologists. After reading this letter, I clambered over the mountains of Ascension with a bounding step and made the volcanic rocks resound under my geological hammer. All this shows how ambitious I was ; but I think that I can say with truth that in after years, though I cared in the highest degree for the approbation of such men as Lyell and Hooker, who were my friends, I did not care much about the general public. I do not mean to say that a favourable review or a large sale of my books did not please me greatly, but the pleasure was a fleeting one, and I am sure that I have never turned one inch out of my course to gain fame.

From my return to England (October 2, 1836) to my marriage (January 29, 1839).

These two years and three months were the most active ones which I ever spent, though I was occasionally unwell, and so lost some time. After going backwards and forwards several times between Shrewsbury, Maer, Cambridge, and London, I settled in lodgings at Cambridge [1] on December 13th, where all my collections were under the care of Henslow. I stayed here three months, and got my minerals and rocks examined by the aid of Professor Miller.

I began preparing my *Journal of Travels*, which was not hard work, as my MS. Journal had been written with care, and my chief labour was making an abstract of my more interesting scientific results. I sent also,

[1] In Fitzwilliam Street.

at the request of Lyell, a short account of my observations on the elevation of the coast of Chili to the Geological Society.[1]

On March 7th, 1837, I took lodgings in Great Marlborough Street in London, and remained there for nearly two years, until I was married. During these two years I finished my Journal, read several papers before the Geological Society, began preparing the MS. for my *Geological Observations*, and arranged for the publication of the *Zoology of the Voyage of the Beagle*. In July I opened my first note-book for facts in relation to the *Origin of Species*, about which I had long reflected, and never ceased working for the next twenty years.

During these two years I also went a little into society, and acted as one of the honorary secretaries of the Geological Society. I saw a great deal of Lyell. One of his chief characteristics was his sympathy with the work of others, and I was as much astonished as delighted at the interest which he showed when, on my return to England, I explained to him my views on coral reefs. This encouraged me greatly, and his advice and example had much influence on me. During this time I saw also a good deal of Robert Brown ; I used often to call and sit with him during his breakfast on Sunday mornings, and he poured forth a rich treasure of curious observations and acute remarks, but they almost always related to minute points, and he never with me discussed large or general questions in science.

During these two years I took several short excursions as a relaxation, and one longer one to the parallel

<hr>

[1] *Geolog. Soc. Proc.* **ii.** 1838, pp. 446–449.

roads of Glen Roy, an account of which was published
in the *Philosophical Transactions*.[1] This paper was
a great failure, and I am ashamed of it. Having
been deeply impressed with what I had seen of the
elevation of the land in South America, I attributed
the parallel lines to the action of the sea ; but I had
to give up this view when Agassiz propounded his
glacier-lake theory. Because no other explanation
was possible under our then state of knowledge, I
argued in favour of sea-action ; and my error has
been a good lesson to me never to trust in science to
the principle of exclusion.

As I was not able to work all day at science, I read
a good deal during these two years on various subjects,
including some metaphysical books ; but I was not
well fitted for such studies. About this time I took
much delight in Wordsworth's and Coleridge's poetry ,
and can boast that I read the *Excursion* twice through.
Formerly Milton's *Paradise Lost* had been my chief
favourite, and in my excursions during the voyage
of the *Beagle*, when I could take only a single volume,
I always chose Milton.

From my marriage, January 29, 1839, *and residence
in Upper Gower Street, to our leaving London and
settling at Down, September* 14, 1842.

[After speaking of his happy married life, and of
his children, he continues :]
During the three years and eight months whilst
we resided in London, I did less scientific work, though
I worked as hard as I possibly could, than during any

[1] 1839, pp. 39–82.

other equal length of time in my life.   This was owing
to frequently recurring unwellness, and to one long
and serious illness.   The greater part of my time,
when I could do anything, was devoted to my work
on *Coral Reefs*, which I had begun before my marriage,
and of which the last proof-sheet was corrected on
May 6th, 1842.   This book, though a small one, cost
me twenty months of hard work, as I had to read
every work on the islands of the Pacific and to consult
many charts.   It was thought highly of by scientific
men, and the theory therein given is, I think, now
well established.

No other work of mine was begun in so deductive
a spirit as this, for the whole theory was thought out
on the west coast of South America, before I had
seen a true coral reef.   I had therefore only to verify
and extend my views by a careful examination of
living reefs.   But it should be observed that I had
during the two previous years been incessantly attending to the effects on the shores of South America
of the intermittent elevation of the land, together
with denudation and the deposition of sediment.
This necessarily led me to reflect much on the effects
of subsidence, and it was easy to replace in imagination the continued deposition of sediment by the
upward growth of corals.   To do this was to form
my theory of the formation of barrier-reefs and
atolls.

Besides my work on coral-reefs, during my residence in London, I read before the Geological Society
papers on the Erratic Boulders of South America,[1]
on Earthquakes,[2] and on the Formation by the

[1] *Geolog. Soc. Proc.* iii. 1842.   [2] *Geolog. Trans.* v. 1840.

Agency of Earth-worms of Mould.[1]   I also continued
to superintend the publication of the *Zoology of the
Voyage of the Beagle.*   Nor did I ever intermit collecting facts bearing on the origin of species ; and I
could sometimes do this when I could do nothing
else from illness.

In the summer of 1842 I was stronger than I had
been for some time, and took a little tour by myself
in North Wales, for the sake of observing the effects
of the old glaciers which formerly filled all the larger
valleys.   I published a short account of what I
saw in the *Philosophical Magazine.*[2]   This excursion
interested me greatly, and it was the last time I was
ever strong enough to climb mountains or to take
long walks such as are necessary for geological work.

During the early part of our life in London, I was
strong enough to go into general society, and saw a
good deal of several scientific men and other more or
less distinguished men.   I will give my impressions
with respect to some of them, though I have little
to say worth saying.

I saw more of Lyell than of any other man, both
before and after my marriage.   His mind was characterised, as it appeared to me, by clearness, caution,
sound judgment, and a good deal of originality.
When I made any remark to him on Geology, he
never rested until he saw the whole case clearly, and
often made me see it more clearly than I had done
before.   He would advance all possible objections to
my suggestion, and even after these were exhausted
would long remain dubious.   A second characteristic

---

[1] *Geolog. Soc. Proc.* ii. 1838.
[2] *Philosophical Magazine,* 1842.

was his hearty sympathy with the work of other scientific men.[1]

On my return from the voyage of the *Beagle*, I explained to him my views on coral-reefs, which differed from his, and I was greatly surprised and encouraged by the vivid interest which he showed. His delight in science was ardent, and he felt the keenest interest in the future progress of mankind. He was very kind-hearted, and thoroughly liberal in his religious beliefs, or rather disbeliefs ; but he was a strong theist. His candour was highly remarkable. He exhibited this by becoming a convert to the Descent theory, though he had gained much fame by opposing Lamarck's views, and this after he had grown old. He reminded me that I had many years before said to him, when discussing the opposition of the old school of geologists to his new views, " What a good thing it would be if every scientific man was to die when sixty years old, as afterwards he would be sure to oppose all new doctrines." But he hoped that now he might be allowed to live.

The science of Geology is enormously indebted to Lyell—more so, as I believe, than to any other man who ever lived. When [I was] starting on the voyage of the *Beagle*, the sagacious Henslow, who, like all other geologists, believed at that time in successive cataclysms, advised me to get and study the first volume of the *Principles*, which had then just been published, but on no account to accept the views

[1] The slight repetition here observable is accounted for by the notes on Lyell, &c., having been added in April, 1881, a few years after the rest of the *Recollections* were written. —F. D.

therein advocated. How differently would any one now speak of the *Principles* ! I am proud to remember that the first place, namely, St. Jago, in the Cape de Verde Archipelago, in which I geologised, convinced me of the infinite superiority of Lyell's views over those advocated in any other work known to me.

The powerful effects of Lyell's works could formerly be plainly seen in the different progress of the science in France and England. The present total oblivion of Elie de Beaumont's wild hypotheses, such as his *Craters of Elevation* and *Lines of Elevation* (which latter hypothesis I heard Sedgwick at the Geological Society lauding to the skies), may be largely attributed to Lyell.

I saw a good deal of Robert Brown, " facile Princeps Botanicorum," as he was called by Humboldt. He seemed to me to be chiefly remarkable for the minuteness of his observations and their perfect accuracy. His knowledge was extraordinarily great, and much died with him, owing to his excessive fear of ever making a mistake. He poured out his knowledge to me in the most unreserved manner, yet was strangely jealous on some points. I called on him two or three times before the voyage of the *Beagle*, and on one occasion he asked me to look through a microscope and describe what I saw. This I did, and believe now that it was the marvellous currents of protoplasm in some vegetable cell. I then asked him what I had seen ; but he answered me, " That is my little secret."

He was capable of the most generous actions. When old, much out of health, and quite unfit for any exertion, he daily visited (as Hooker told me) an old man-servant, who lived at a distance (and whom he supported), and read aloud to him.   This is enough to make up for any degree of scientific penuriousness or jealousy.

I may here mention a few other eminent men whom I have occasionally seen, but I have little to say about them worth saying.   I felt a high reverence for Sir J. Herschel, and was delighted to dine with him at his charming house at the Cape of Good Hope and afterwards at his London house.   I saw him, also, on a few other occasions.   He never talked much, but every word which he uttered was worth listening to.

I once met at breakfast, at Sir R. Murchison's house, the illustrious Humboldt, who honoured me by expressing a wish to see me.   I was a little disappointed with the great man, but my anticipations probably were too high.   I can remember nothing distinctly about our interview, except that Humboldt was very cheerful and talked much.

X.[1] reminds me of Buckle, whom I once met at Hensleigh Wedgwood's.   I was very glad to learn from [Buckle] his system of collecting facts.   He told me that he bought all the books which he read, and made a full index to each, of the facts which he thought might prove serviceable to him, and that he could always remember in what book he had read anything, for his memory was wonderful.   I asked him how at first he could judge what facts would be serviceable, and he answered that he did not know, but that a sort of instinct guided him.   From this habit of

[1] A passage referring to X. is here omitted.—F. D.

making indices, he was enabled to give the astonishing number of references on all sorts of subjects which may be found in his *History of Civilisation*. This book I thought most interesting, and read it twice, but I doubt whether his generalisations are worth anything. Buckle was a great talker ; and I listened to him, saying hardly a word, nor indeed could I have done so, for he left no gaps. When Mrs. Farrer began to sing, I jumped up and said that I must listen to her. After I had moved away, he turned round to a friend, and said (as was overheard by my brother), " Well, Mr. Darwin's books are much better than his conversation."

Of other great literary men, I once met Sydney Smith at Dean Milman's house. There was something inexplicably amusing in every word which he uttered. Perhaps this was partly due to the expectation of being amused. He was talking about Lady Cork, who was then extremely old. This was the lady who, as he said, was once so much affected by one of his charity sermons, that she *borrowed* a guinea from a friend to put in the plate. He now said, " It is generally believed that my dear old friend Lady Cork has been overlooked " ; and he said this in such a manner that no one could for a moment doubt that he meant that his dear old friend had been overlooked by the devil. How he managed to express this I know not.

I likewise once met Macaulay at Lord Stanhope's (the historian's) house, and as there was only one other man at dinner, I had a grand opportunity of hearing him converse, and he was very agreeable. He did not talk at all too much, nor indeed could such a man talk too much, as long as he allowed others to turn the stream of his conversation, and this he did allow.

Lord Stanhope once gave me a curious little proof of the accuracy and fulness of Macaulay's memory. Many historians used often to meet at Lord Stanhope's house ; and, in discussing various subjects, they would sometimes differ from Macaulay, and formerly they often referred to some book to see who was right ; but latterly, as Lord Stanhope noticed, no historian ever took this trouble, and whatever Macaulay said was final.

On another occasion I met at Lord Stanhope's house one of his parties of historians and other literary men, and amongst them were Motley and Grote. After luncheon I walked about Chevening Park for nearly an hour with Grote, and was much interested by his conversation and pleased by the simplicity and absence of all pretension in his manners.

Long ago I dined occasionally with the old Earl, the father of the historian. He was a strange man, but what little I knew of him I liked much. He was frank, genial, and pleasant. He had strongly-marked features, with a brown complexion, and his clothes, when I saw him, were all brown. He seemed to believe in everything which was to others utterly incredible. He said one day to me, " Why don't you give up your fiddle-faddle of geology and zoology, and turn to the occult sciences ? " The historian, then Lord Mahon, seemed shocked at such a speech to me, and his charming wife much amused.

The last man whom I will mention is Carlyle, seen by me several times at my brother's house and two or three times at my own house. His talk was very racy and interesting, just like his writings, but he sometimes went on too long on the same subject. I remember a funny dinner at my brother's, where, amongst a few others, were Babbage and Lyell, both of whom liked to talk. Carlyle, however, silenced every one by haranguing during the whole dinner on the advantages of silence. After dinner, Babbage, in his grimmest manner, thanked Carlyle for his very interesting lecture on silence.

Carlyle sneered at almost every one : One day in my house he called Grote's *History* " a fetid quagmire, with nothing spiritual about it." I always thought, until his *Reminiscences* appeared, that his sneers were partly jokes, but this now seems rather doubtful. His expression was that of a depressed, almost despondent, yet benevolent man, and it is notorious how heartily he laughed. I believe that his benevolence was real, though stained by not a little jealousy. No one can doubt about his extraordinary power of drawing pictures of things and men—far more vivid, as it appears to me, than any drawn by Macaulay. Whether his pictures of men were true ones is another question.

He has been all-powerful in impressing some grand moral truths on the minds of men. On the other hand, his views about slavery were revolting. In his eyes might was right. His mind seemed to me a very narrow one ; even if all branches of science, which he despised, are excluded. It is astonishing to me that Kingsley should have spoken of him as a man well fitted to advance science. He laughed to scorn the idea that a mathematician, such as

Whewell, could judge, as I maintained he could, of Goethe's views on light. He thought it a most ridiculous thing that any one should care whether a glacier moved a little quicker or a little slower, or moved at all. As far as I could judge, I never met a man with a mind so ill adapted for scientific research.

Whilst living in London, I attended as regularly as I could the meetings of several scientific societies, and acted as secretary to the Geological Society. But such attendance, and ordinary society, suited my health so badly that we resolved to live in the country, which we both preferred and have never repented of.

Residence at Down, from September 14, 1842, *to the present time,* 1876.

After several fruitless searches in Surrey and elsewhere, we found this house and purchased it. I was pleased with the diversified appearance of the vegetation proper to a chalk district, and so unlike what I had been accustomed to in the Midland counties ; and still more pleased with the extreme quietness and rusticity of the place. It is not, however, quite so retired a place as a writer in a German periodical makes it, who says that my house can be approached only by a mule-track ! Our fixing ourselves here has answered admirably in one way which we did not anticipate, namely, by being very convenient for frequent visits from our children.

Few persons can have lived a more retired life than we have done. Besides short visits to the houses of relations, and occasionally to the seaside or else-

AUTOBIOGRAPHY OF CHARLES DARWIN

where, we have gone nowhere. During the first part
of our residence we went a little into society, and
received a few friends here ; but my health almost
always suffered from the excitement, violent shivering
and vomiting attacks being thus brought on. I have
therefore been compelled for many years to give up
all dinner-parties ; and this has been somewhat of
a deprivation to me, as such parties always put me
into high spirits. From the same cause I have been
able to invite here very few scientific acquaintances.

My chief enjoyment and sole employment throughout life has been scientific work, and the excitement
from such work makes me for the time forget, or drives
quite away, my daily discomfort. I have therefore
nothing to record during the rest of my life, except
the publication of my several books. Perhaps a few
details how they arose may be worth giving.

My several Publications.—In the early part of 1844,
my observations on the volcanic islands visited during
the voyage of the *Beagle* were published. In 1845,
I took much pains in correcting a new edition of
my *Journal of Researches*, which was originally published in 1839 as part of Fitz-Roy's work. The
success of this my first literary child always tickles
my vanity more than that of any of my other books.
Even to this day it sells steadily in England and the
United States, and has been translated for the second
time into German, and into French and other languages. This success of a book of travels, especially
of a scientific one, so many years after its first publication, is surprising. Ten thousand copies have been
sold in England of the second edition. In 1846
my *Geological Observations on South America* were

published. I record in a little diary, which I have always kept, that my three geological books (*Coral Reefs* included) consumed four and a half years' steady work ; " and now it is ten years since my return to England, How much time have I lost by illness ? " I have nothing to say about these three books except that to my surprise new editions have lately been called for.[1]

In October, 1846, I began to work on ' Cirripedia ' (Barnacles). When on the coast of Chile, I found a most curious form, which burrowed into shells of Concholepas, and which differed so much from all other Cirripedes that I had to form a new sub-order for its sole reception. Lately an allied burrowing genus has been found on the shores of Portugal. To understand the structure of my new Cirripede I had to examine and dissect many of the common forms : and this gradually led me on to take up the whole group. I worked steadily on the subject for the next eight years, and ultimately published two thick volumes,[2] describing all the known living species, and two thin quartos on the extinct species. I do not doubt that Sir E. Lytton Bulwer had me in his mind when he introduced in one of his novels a Professor Long, who had written two huge volumes on limpets.

Although I was employed during eight years on this work, yet I record in my diary that about two years out of this time was lost by illness. On this account I went in 1848 for some months to Malvern

[1] *Geological Observations*, 2nd Edit. 1876. *Coral Reefs*, 2nd Edit. 1874.

[2] Published by the Ray Society.

for hydropathic treatment, which did me much good, so that on my return home I was able to resume work. So much was I out of health that when my dear father died on November 13th, 1848, I was unable to attend his funeral or to act as one of his executors.

My work on the Cirripedia possesses, I think, considerable value, as besides describing several new and remarkable forms, I made out the homologies of the various parts—I discovered the cementing apparatus, though I blundered dreadfully about the cement glands—and lastly I proved the existence in certain genera of minute males complemental to and parasitic on the hermaphrodites. This latter discovery has at last been fully confirmed ; though at one time a German writer was pleased to attribute the whole account to my fertile imagination. The Cirripedes form a highly varying and difficult group of species to class ; and my work was of considerable use to me, when I had to discuss in the *Origin of Species* the principles of a natural classification. Nevertheless, I doubt whether the work was worth the consumption of so much time.

From September 1854 I devoted my whole time to arranging my huge pile of notes, to observing, and to experimenting in relation to the transmutation of species. During the voyage of the *Beagle* I had been deeply impressed by discovering in the Pampean formation great fossil animals covered with armour like that on the existing armadillos ; secondly, by the manner in which closely allied animals replace one another in proceeding southwards over the Continent ; and thirdly, by the South American character of most of the productions of the Galapagos archipelago, and more especially by the manner in which they differ slightly on each island of the group ; none of the islands appearing to be very ancient in a geological sense.

It was evident that such facts as these, as well as many others, could only be explained on the supposition that species gradually become modified ; and the subject haunted me. But it was equally evident that neither the action of the surrounding conditions, nor the will of the organisms (especially in the case of plants), could account for the innumerable cases in which organisms of every kind are beautifully adapted to their habits of life—for instance, a woodpecker or a tree-frog to climb trees, or a seed for dispersal by hooks or plumes. I had always been much struck by such adaptations, and until these could be explained it seemed to me almost useless to endeavour to prove by indirect evidence that species have been modified.

After my return to England it appeared to me that by following the example of Lyell in Geology, and by collecting all facts which bore in any way on the variation of animals and plants under domestication and nature, some light might perhaps be thrown on the whole subject. My first note-book was opened in July 1837. I worked on true Baconian principles, and without any theory collected facts on a wholesale scale, more especially with respect to domesticated productions, by printed enquiries, by conversation with skilful breeders and gardeners, and by extensive reading. When I see the list of books of all kinds which I read and abstracted, including whole series of Journals and Transactions, I am surprised at my industry. I soon perceived that selection was the keystone of man's success in making useful races of animals and plants. But how selection could be applied to organisms living in a state of nature remained for some time a mystery to me.

In October 1838, that is, fifteen months after I had begun my systematic enquiry, I happened to read for amusement Malthus on *Population*, and being well prepared to appreciate the struggle for existence which everywhere goes on from long-continued observation of the habits of animals and plants, it at once struck me that under these circumstances favourable variations would tend to be preserved, and unfavourable ones to be destroyed. The result of this would be the formation of new species. Here, then, I had at last got a theory by which to work ; but I was so anxious to avoid prejudice, that I determined not for some time to write even the briefest sketch of it. In June 1842 I first allowed myself the satisfaction of writing a very brief abstract of my theory in pencil in 35 pages ; and this was enlarged during the summer of 1844 into one of 230 pages, which I had fairly copied out and still possess.

But at that time I overlooked one problem of great importance ; and it is astonishing to me, except on the principle of Columbus and his egg, how I could have overlooked it and its solution. This problem is the tendency in organic beings descended from the same stock to diverge in character as they become modified. That they have diverged greatly is obvious from the manner in which species of all kinds can be classed under genera, genera under families, families under sub-orders, and so forth ; and I can remember the very spot in the road, whilst in my carriage, when to my joy the solution occurred to me ; and this was long after I had come to Down. The solution, as I believe, is that the modified offspring of all dominant and increasing forms tend to become adapted to many and highly diversified places in the economy of nature.

Early in 1856 Lyell advised me to write out my views pretty fully, and I began at once to do so on a scale three or four times as extensive as that which was afterwards followed in my *Origin of Species* ; yet it was only an abstract of the materials which I had collected, and I got through about half the work on this scale. But my plans were overthrown, for early in the summer of 1858 Mr. Wallace, who was then in the Malay archipelago, sent me an essay *On the Tendency of Varieties to depart indefinitely from the Original Type* ; and this essay contained exactly the same theory as mine. Mr. Wallace expressed the wish that if I thought well of his essay, I should send it to Lyell for perusal.

The circumstances under which I consented at the request of Lyell and Hooker to allow of an abstract from my MS., together with a letter to Asa Gray, dated September 5, 1857, to be published at the same time with Wallace's Essay, are given in the *Journal of the Proceedings of the Linnean Society*, 1858, p. 45. I was at first very unwilling to consent, as I thought Mr. Wallace might consider my doing so unjustifiable, for I did not then know how generous and noble was his disposition. The extract from my MS. and the letter to Asa Gray had neither been intended for publication, and were badly written.

Mr. Wallace's essay, on the other hand, was admirably expressed and quite clear. Nevertheless, our joint productions excited very little attention, and the only published notice of them which I can remember was by Professor Haughton of Dublin, whose verdict was that all that was new in them was false, and what was true was old. This shows how necessary it is that any new view should be explained at considerable length in order to arouse public attention.

In September 1858 I set to work by the strong advice of Lyell and Hooker to prepare a volume on the transmutation of species, but was often interrupted by ill-health, and short visits to Dr. Lane's delightful hydropathic establishment at Moor Park. I abstracted the MS. begun on a much larger scale in 1856, and completed the volume on the same reduced scale. It cost me thirteen months and ten days' hard labour. It was published under the title of the *Origin of Species*, in November 1859. Though considerably added to and corrected in the later editions, it has remained substantially the same book.

It is no doubt the chief work of my life. It was from the first highly successful. The first small edition of 1250 copies was sold on the day of publication, and a second edition of 3000 copies soon afterwards. Sixteen thousand copies have now (1876) been sold in England ; and considering how stiff a book it is, this is a large sale. It has been translated into almost every European tongue, even into such languages as Spanish, Bohemian, Polish, and Russian. It has also, according to Miss Bird, been translated into Japanese,[1] and is there much studied. Even an essay in Hebrew has appeared on it, showing that the theory is contained in the Old Testament ! The reviews were very numerous ; for some time I collected all that appeared on the *Origin* and on my related books, and these amount (excluding newspaper reviews) to 265 ; but after a time I gave up the attempt in despair. Many separate essays and books on the subject have appeared ; and in Germany a catalogue or bibliography on " Darwinismus " has appeared every year or two.

The success of the *Origin* may, I think, be attributed in large part to my having long before written two condensed sketches, and to my having finally abstracted a much larger manuscript, which was itself an abstract. By this means I was enabled to select the more striking facts and conclusions. I had, also, during many years, followed a golden rule, namely, that whenever a published fact, a new observation or thought came across me, which was opposed to my general results, to make a memorandum of it without fail and at once ; for I had found by experience that such facts and thoughts were far more apt to escape from the memory than favourable ones. Owing to this habit, very few objections were raised against my views which I had not at least noticed and attempted to answer.

It has sometimes been said that the success of the *Origin* proved " that the subject was in the air," or " that men's minds were prepared for it." I do not think that this is strictly true, for I occasionally

[1] Miss Bird is mistaken, as I learn from Professor Mitsukuri. —F. D.

sounded not a few naturalists, and never happened to come across a single one who seemed to doubt about the permanence of species. Even Lyell and Hooker, though they would listen with interest to me, never seemed to agree. I tried once or twice to explain to able men what I meant by Natural selection, but signally failed. What I believe was strictly true is that innumerable well-observed facts were stored in the minds of naturalists ready to take their proper places as soon as any theory which would receive them was sufficiently explained. Another element in the success of the book was its moderate size ; and this I owe to the appearance of Mr. Wallace's essay ; had I published on the scale in which I began to write in 1856, the book would have been four or five times as large as the *Origin*, and very few would have had the patience to read it.

I gained much by my delay in publishing from about 1839, when the theory was clearly conceived, to 1859 ; and I lost nothing by it, for I cared very little whether men attributed most originality to me or Wallace ; and his essay no doubt aided in the reception of the theory. I was forestalled in only one important point, which my vanity has always made me regret, namely, the explanation by means of the Glacial period of the presence of the same species of plants and of some few animals on distant mountain summits and in the arctic regions. This view pleased me so much that I wrote it out *in extenso*, and I believe that it was read by Hooker some years before E. Forbes published his celebrated memoir [1] on the subject. In the very few points in which we

[1] *Geolog. Survey Mem.*, 1846.

differed, I still think that I was in the right. I have never, of course, alluded in print to my having independently worked out this view.

Hardly any point gave me so much satisfaction when I was at work on the *Origin*, as the explanation of the wide difference in many classes between the embryo and the adult animal, and of the close resemblance of the embryos within the same class. No notice of this point was taken, as far as I remember, in the early reviews of the *Origin*, and I recollect expressing my surprise on this head in a letter to Asa Gray. Within late years several reviewers have given the whole credit to Fritz Müller and Häckel, who undoubtedly have worked it out much more fully, and in some respects more correctly than I did. I had materials for a whole chapter on the subject, and I ought to have made the discussion longer ; for it is clear that I failed to impress my readers ; and he who succeeds in doing so deserves, in my opinion, all the credit.

This leads me to remark that I have almost always been treated honestly by my reviewers, passing over those without scientific knowledge as not worthy of notice. My views have often been grossly misrepresented, bitterly opposed and ridiculed, but this has been generally done, as I believe, in good faith. On the whole I do not doubt that my works have been over and over again greatly overpraised. I rejoice that I have avoided controversies, and this I owe to Lyell, who many years ago, in reference to my geological works, strongly advised me never to get entangled in a controversy, as it rarely did any good and caused a miserable loss of time and temper.

Whenever I have found out that I have blundered, or that my work has been imperfect, and when I have been contemptuously criticised, and even when I have been overpraised, so that I have felt mortified, it has been my greatest comfort to say hundreds of times to myself that " I have worked as hard and as well as I could, and no man can do more than this." I remember when in Good Success Bay, in Tierra del Fuego, thinking (and, I believe, that I wrote home to the effect) that I could not employ my life better than in adding a little to Natural Science. This I have done to the best of my abilities, and critics may say what they like, but they cannot destroy this conviction.

During the two last months of 1859 I was fully occupied in preparing a second edition of the *Origin*, and by an enormous correspondence. On January 1st, 1860, I began arranging my notes for my work on the *Variation of Animals and Plants under Domestication* ; but it was not published until the beginning of 1868 ; the delay having been caused partly by frequent illnesses, one of which lasted seven months, and partly by being tempted to publish on other subjects which at the time interested me more.

On May 15th, 1862, my little book on the *Fertilisation of Orchids*, which cost me ten months' work, was published : most of the facts had been slowly accumulated during several previous years. During the summer of 1839, and, I believe, during the previous summer, I was led to attend to the cross-fertilisation of flowers by the aid of insects, from having come to the conclusion in my speculations on the origin of species, that crossing played an important part in

63

keeping specific forms constant. I attended to the subject more or less during every subsequent summer; and my interest in it was greatly enhanced by having procured and read in November 1841, through the advice of Robert Brown, a copy of C. K. Sprengel's wonderful book, *Das entdeckte Geheimniss der Natur*. For some years before 1862 I had specially attended to the fertilisation of our British orchids; and it seemed to me the best plan to prepare as complete a treatise on this group of plants as well as I could, rather than to utilise the great mass of matter which I had slowly collected with respect to other plants.

My resolve proved a wise one; for since the appearance of my book, a surprising number of papers and separate works on the fertilisation of all kinds of flowers have appeared; and these are far better done than I could possibly have effected. The merits of poor old Sprengel, so long overlooked, are now fully recognised many years after his death.

During the same year I published in the *Journal of the Linnean Society*, a paper *On the Two Forms, or Dimorphic Condition of Primula*, and during the next five years, five other papers on dimorphic and trimorphic plants. I do not think anything in my scientific life has given me so much satisfaction as making out the meaning of the structure of these plants. I had noticed in 1838 or 1839 the dimorphism of *Linum flavum*, and had at first thought that it was merely a case of unmeaning variability. But on examining the common species of Primula, I found that the two forms were much too regular and constant to be thus viewed. I therefore became almost convinced that the common cowslip and prim-

rose were on the high-road to become diœcious ;—
that the short pistil in the one form, and the short
stamens in the other form were tending towards
abortion. The plants were therefore subjected under
this point of view to trial ; but as soon as the flowers
with short pistils fertilised with pollen from the short
stamens, were found to yield more seeds than any
other of the four possible unions, the abortion-theory
was knocked on the head. After some additional
experiment, it became evident that the two forms,
though both were perfect hermaphrodites, bore almost
the same relation to one another as do the two sexes
of an ordinary animal. With Lythrum we have the
still more wonderful case of three forms standing
in a similar relation to one another. I afterwards
found that the offspring from the union of two plants
belonging to the same forms presented a close and
curious analogy with hybrids from the union of two
distinct species.

In the autumn of 1864 I finished a long paper on
Climbing Plants, and sent it to the Linnean Society.
The writing of this paper cost me four months : but
I was so unwell when I received the proof-sheets that
I was forced to leave them very badly and often
obscurely expressed. The paper was little noticed,
but when in 1875 it was corrected and published as
a separate book it sold well. I was led to take up
this subject by reading a short paper by Asa Gray,
published in 1858. He sent me seeds, and on raising
some plants I was so much fascinated and perplexed
by the revolving movements of the tendrils and stems,
which movements are really very simple, though
appearing at first sight very complex, that I procured

various other kinds of climbing plants, and studied the whole subject. I was all the more attracted to it, from not being at all satisfied with the explanation which Henslow gave us in his lectures, about twining plants, namely, that they had a natural tendency to grow up in a spire. This explanation proved quite erroneous. Some of the adaptations displayed by climbing plants are as beautiful as those of Orchids for ensuring cross-fertilisation.

My *Variation of Animals and Plants under Domestication* was begun, as already stated, in the beginning of 1860, but was not published until the beginning of 1868. It was a big book, and cost me four years and two months' hard labour. It gives all my observations and an immense number of facts collected from various sources, about our domestic productions. In the second volume the causes and laws of variation, inheritance, &c., are discussed, as far as our present state of knowledge permits. Towards the end of the work I give my well-abused hypothesis of Pangenesis. An unverified hypothesis is of little or no value ; but if any one should hereafter be led to make observations by which some such hypothesis could be established, I shall have done good service, as an astonishing number of isolated facts can be thus connected together and rendered intelligible. In 1875 a second and largely corrected edition, which cost me a good deal of labour, was brought out.

My *Descent of Man* was published in February 1871. As soon as I had become, in the year 1837 or 1838, convinced that species were mutable productions, I could not avoid the belief that man must come under the same law. Accordingly I collected notes on the subject for my own satisfaction, and not for a long time with any intention of publishing. Although in the *Origin of Species* the derivation of any particular species is never discussed, yet I thought it best, in order that no honourable man should accuse me of concealing my views, to add that by the work " light would be thrown on the origin of man and his history." It would have been useless, and injurious to the success of the book, to have paraded, without giving any evidence, my conviction with respect to his origin.

But when I found that many naturalists fully accepted the doctrine of the evolution of species, it seemed to me advisable to work up such notes as I possessed, and to publish a special treatise on the origin of man. I was the more glad to do so, as it gave me an opportunity of fully discussing sexual selection—a subject which had always greatly interested me. This subject, and that of the variation of our domestic productions, together with the causes and laws of variation, inheritance, and the intercrossing of plants, are the sole subjects which I have been able to write about in full, so as to use all the materials which I have collected. The *Descent of Man* took me three years to write, but then as usual some of this time was lost by ill health, and some was consumed by preparing new editions and other minor works. A second and largely corrected edition of the *Descent* appeared in 1874.

My book on the *Expression of the Emotions in Men and Animals* was published in the autumn of 1872. I had intended to give only a chapter on the subject in the *Descent of Man*, but as soon as I began to put my notes together, I saw that it would require a separate treatise.

My first child was born on December 27th, 1839, and I at once commenced to make notes on the first dawn of the various expressions which he exhibited, for I felt convinced, even at this early period, that the most complex and fine shades of expression must all have had a gradual and natural origin. During the summer of the following year, 1840, I read Sir C. Bell's admirable work on expression, and this greatly increased the interest which I felt in the subject, though I could not at all agree with his belief that various muscles had been specially created for the sake of expression. From this time forward I occasionally attended to the subject, both with respect to man and our domesticated animals. My book sold largely ; 5267 copies having been disposed of on the day of publication.

In the summer of 1860 I was idling and resting near Hartfield, where two species of [Sundew] abound ; and I noticed that numerous insects had been entrapped by the leaves. I carried home some plants, and on giving them insects saw the movements of the tentacles, and this made me think it probable that the insects were caught for some special purpose. Fortunately a crucial test occurred to me, that of placing a large number of leaves in various nitrogenous and non-nitrogenous fluids of equal density ; and as soon as I found that the former alone excited energetic movements, it was obvious that here was a fine new field for investigation.

During subsequent years, whenever I had leisure, I pursued my experiments, and my book on *Insecti-*

vorous Plants was published in July 1875—that is sixteen years after my first observations. The delay
in this case, as with all my other books, has been a
great advantage to me ; for a man after a long interval
can criticise his own work, almost as well as if it were
that of another person. The fact that a plant should
secrete, when properly excited, a fluid containing an
acid and ferment, closely analogous to the digestive
fluid of an animal, was certainly a remarkable discovery.

During this autumn of 1876 I shall publish on the
*Effects of Cross- and Self-Fertilisation in the Vegetable
Kingdom.* This book will form a complement to that
on the *Fertilisation of Orchids,* in which I showed how
perfect were the means for cross-fertilisation, and here
I shall show how important are the results. I was
led to make, during eleven years, the numerous experiments recorded in this volume, by a mere accidental
observation ; and indeed it required the accident to
be repeated before my attention was thoroughly
aroused to the remarkable fact that seedlings of self-
fertilised parentage are inferior, even in the first
generation, in height and vigour to seedlings of cross-
fertilised parentage. I hope also to republish a
revised edition of my book on Orchids, and hereafter
my papers on dimorphic and trimorphic plants,
together with some additional observations on allied
points which I never have had time to arrange. My
strength will then probably be exhausted, and I shall
be ready to exclaim " Nunc dimittis."

*Written May 1st, 1881.—The Effects of Cross- and
Self-Fertilisation* was published in the autumn of
1876 ; and the results there arrived at explain, as I

believe, the endless and wonderful contrivances for the transportal of pollen from one plant to another of the same species. I now believe, however, chiefly from the observations of Hermann Müller, that I ought to have insisted more strongly than I did on the many adaptations for self-fertilisation ; though I was well aware of many such adaptations. A much enlarged edition of my *Fertilisation of Orchids* was published in 1877.

In this same year *The Different Forms of Flowers, &c.*, appeared, and in 1880 a second edition. This book consists chiefly of the several papers on hetero-styled flowers originally published by the Linnean Society, corrected, with much new matter added, together with observations on some other cases in which the same plant bears two kinds of flowers. As before remarked, no little discovery of mine ever gave me so much pleasure as the making out the meaning of hetero-styled flowers. The results of crossing such flowers in an illegitimate manner, I believe to be very important, as bearing on the sterility of hybrids ; although these results have been noticed by only a few persons.

In 1879, I had a translation of Dr. Ernst Krause's *Life of Erasmus Darwin* published, and I added a sketch of his character and habits from material in my possession. Many persons have been much interested by this little life, and I am surprised that only 800 or 900 copies were sold.

In 1880 I published, with [my son] Frank's assistance, our *Power of Movement in Plants*. This was a tough piece of work. The book bears somewhat the same relation to my little book on *Climbing Plants,* which *Cross-Fertilisation* did to the *Fertilisation of Orchids* ; for in accordance with the principle of evolution it was impossible to account for climbing plants having been developed in so many widely different groups unless all kinds of plants possess some slight power of movement of an analogous kind. This I proved to be the case ; and I was further led to a rather wide generalisation, viz., that the great and important classes of movements, excited by light, the attraction of gravity, &c., are all modified forms of the fundamental movement of circumnutation. It has always pleased me to exalt plants in the scale of organised beings ; and I therefore felt an especial pleasure in showing how many and what admirably well adapted movements the tip of a root possesses.

I have now (May 1, 1881) sent to the printers the MS. of a little book on *The Formation of Vegetable Mould through the Action of Worms.* This is a subject of but small importance ; and I know not whether it will interest any readers,[1] but it has interested me. It is the completion of a short paper read before the Geological Society more than forty years ago, and has revived old geological thoughts.

I have now mentioned all the books which I have published, and these have been the milestones in my life, so that little remains to be said. I am not conscious of any change in my mind during the last thirty years, excepting in one point presently to be mentioned ; nor, indeed, could any change have been expected unless one of general deterioration. But

[1] Between November 1881 and February 1884, 8500 copies were sold.—F. D.

my father lived to his eighty-third year with his mind as lively as ever it was, and all his faculties undimmed; and I hope that I may die before my mind fails to a sensible extent. I think that I have become a little more skilful in guessing right explanations and in devising experimental tests; but this may probably be the result of mere practice, and of a larger store of knowledge. I have as much difficulty as ever in expressing myself clearly and concisely; and this difficulty has caused me a very great loss of time; but it has had the compensating advantage of forcing me to think long and intently about every sentence, and thus I have been led to see errors in reasoning and in my own observations or those of others.

There seems to be a sort of fatality in my mind leading me to put at first my statement or proposition in a wrong or awkward form. Formerly I used to think about my sentences before writing them down; but for several years I have found that it saves time to scribble in a vile hand, whole pages as quickly as I possibly can, contracting half the words; and then correct deliberately. Sentences thus scribbled down are often better ones than I could have written deliberately.

Having said thus much about my manner of writing, I will add that with my large books I spend a good deal of time over the general arrangement of the matter. I first make the rudest outline in two or three pages, and then a larger one in several pages, a few words or one word standing for a whole discussion or series of facts. Each one of these headings is again enlarged and often transferred before I begin to

write *in extenso*. As in several of my books facts
observed by others have been very extensively used,
and as I have always had several quite distinct subjects in hand at the same time, I may mention that I
keep from thirty to forty large portfolios, in cabinets
with labelled shelves, into which I can at once put
a detached reference or memorandum. I have bought
many books, and at their ends I make an index of all
the facts that concern my work ; or, if the book is
not my own, write out a separate abstract, and of such
abstracts I have a large drawer full. Before beginning
on any subject I look to all the short indexes and make
a general and classified index, and by taking the one
or more proper portfolios I have all the information
collected during my life ready for use.

I have said that in one respect my mind has changed
during the last twenty or thirty years. Up to the age
of thirty, or beyond it, poetry of many kinds, such
as the works of Milton, Gray, Byron, Wordsworth,
Coleridge, and Shelley, gave me great pleasure, and
even as a schoolboy I took intense delight in Shakespeare, especially in the historical plays. I have also
said that formerly pictures gave me considerable, and
music very great delight. But now for many years
I cannot endure to read a line of poetry : I have
tried lately to read Shakespeare, and found it so
intolerably dull that it nauseated me. I have also
almost lost my taste for pictures or music. Music
generally sets me thinking too energetically on what
I have been at work on, instead of giving me pleasure.
I retain some taste for fine scenery, but it does not
cause me the exquisite delight which it formerly did.
On the other hand, novels, which are works of the

imagination, though not of a very high order, have been for years a wonderful relief and pleasure to me, and I often bless all novelists. A surprising number have been read aloud to me, and I like all if moderately good, and if they do not end unhappily—against which a law ought to be passed. A novel, according to my taste, does not come into the first class unless it contains some person whom one can thoroughly love, and if a pretty woman all the better.

This curious and lamentable loss of the higher æsthetic tastes is all the odder, as books on history, biographies, and travels (independently of any scientific facts which they may contain), and essays on all sorts of subjects interest me as much as ever they did. My mind seems to have become a kind of machine for grinding general laws out of large collections of facts, but why this should have caused the atrophy of that part of the brain alone, on which the higher tastes depend, I cannot conceive. A man with a mind more highly organised or better constituted than mine, would not, I suppose, have thus suffered ; and if I had to live my life again, I would have made a rule to read some poetry and listen to some music at least once every week ; for perhaps the parts of my brain now atrophied would thus have been kept active through use. The loss of these tastes is a loss of happiness, and may possibly be injurious to the intellect, and more probably to the moral character, by enfeebling the emotional part of our nature.

My books have sold largely in England, have been translated into many languages, and passed through several editions in foreign countries. I have heard it said that the success of a work abroad is the best test of its enduring value. I doubt whether this is at all trustworthy ; but judged by this standard my name ought to last for a few years. Therefore it may be worth while to try to analyse the mental qualities and the conditions on which my success has depended ; though I am aware that no man can do this correctly.

I have no great quickness of apprehension or wit which is so remarkable in some clever men, for instance, Huxley. I am therefore a poor critic : a paper or book, when first read, generally excites my admiration, and it is only after considerable reflection that I perceive the weak points. My power to follow a long and purely abstract train of thought is very limited ; and therefore I could never have succeeded with metaphysics or mathematics. My memory is extensive, yet hazy : it suffices to make me cautious by vaguely telling me that I have observed or read something opposed to the conclusion which I am drawing, or on the other hand in favour of it ; and after a time I can generally recollect where to search for my authority. So poor in one sense is my memory, that I have never been able to remember for more than a few days a single date or a line of poetry.

Some of my critics have said, " Oh, he is a good observer, but he has no power of reasoning ! " I do not think that this can be true, for the *Origin of Species* is one long argument from the beginning to the end, and it has convinced not a few able men. No one could have written it without having some power of reasoning. I have a fair share of invention, and of common sense or judgment, such as every fairly successful lawyer or doctor must have, but not, I believe, in any higher degree.

On the favourable side of the balance, I think that I am superior to the common run of men in noticing things which easily escape attention, and in observing them carefully. My industry has been nearly as great as it could have been in the observation and collection of facts. What is far more important, my love of natural science has been steady and ardent.

This pure love has, however, been much aided by the ambition to be esteemed by my fellow naturalists. From my early youth I have had the strongest desire to understand or explain whatever I observed, —that is, to group all facts under some general laws. These causes combined have given me the patience to reflect or ponder for any number of years over any unexplained problem. As far as I can judge, I am not apt to follow blindly the lead of other men. I have steadily endeavoured to keep my mind free so as to give up any hypothesis, however much beloved (and I cannot resist forming one on every subject), as soon as facts are shown to be opposed to it. Indeed, I have had no choice but to act in this manner, for with the exception of the Coral Reefs, I cannot remember a single first-formed hypothesis which had not after a time to be given up or greatly modified. This has naturally led me to distrust greatly, deductive reasoning in the mixed sciences. On the other hand, I am not very sceptical,—a frame of mind which I believe to be injurious to the progress of science. A good deal of scepticism in a scientific man is advisable to avoid much loss of time, [but] I have met with not a few men, who, I feel sure, have often thus been deterred from experiment or observations, which would have proved directly or indirectly serviceable.

In illustration, I will give the oddest case which I have known. A gentleman (who, as I afterwards heard, is a good local botanist) wrote to me from the Eastern counties that the seeds or beans of the common field-bean had this year everywhere grown on the wrong side of the pod. I wrote back, asking for further information, as I did not understand what was meant ; but I did not receive any answer for a very long time. I then saw in two newspapers, one published in Kent and the other in Yorkshire, paragraphs stating that it was a most remarkable fact that " the beans this year had all grown on the wrong side." So I thought there must be some foundation for so general a statement. Accordingly, I went to my gardener, an old Kentish man, and asked him whether he had heard anything about it, and he answered, " Oh, no, sir, it must be a mistake, for the beans grow on the wrong side only on leap-year." I then asked him how they grew in common years and how on leap-years, but soon found that he knew absolutely nothing of how they grew at any time, but he stuck to his belief.

After a time I heard from my first informant, who, with many apologies, said that he should not have written to me had he not heard the statement from several intelligent farmers ; but that he had since spoken again to every one of them, and not one knew in the least what he had himself meant. So that here a belief—if indeed a statement with no definite idea attached to it can be called a belief—had spread over almost the whole of England without any vestige of evidence.

I have known in the course of my life only three intentionally falsified statements, and one of these may have been a hoax (and there have been several scientific hoaxes) which, however, took in an American agricultural journal. It related to the formation in Holland of a new breed of oxen by the crossing of distinct species of Bos (some of which I happen to know are sterile together), and the author had the impudence to state that he had corresponded with me, and that I had been deeply impressed with the importance of his result. The article was sent to me by the editor of an English agricultural journal, asking for my opinion before republishing it.

A second case was an account of several varieties, raised by the author from several species of Primula, which had spontaneously yielded a full complement of seed, although the parent plants had been carefully protected from the access of insects. This account was published before I had discovered the meaning of heterostylism, and the whole statement must have been fraudulent, or there was neglect in excluding insects so gross as to be scarcely credible.

The third case was more curious : Mr. Huth published in his book on ' Consanguineous Marriage ' some long extracts from a Belgian author, who stated that he had interbred rabbits in the closest manner for very many generations, without the least injurious effects. The account was published in a most respectable Journal, that of the Royal Society of Belgium ; but I could not avoid feeling doubts—I hardly know why, except that there were no accidents of any kind, and my experience in breeding animals made me think this improbable.

So with much hesitation I wrote to Professor Van Beneden, asking him whether the author was a trustworthy man. I soon heard in answer that the Society had been greatly shocked by discovering that the whole account was a fraud.[1] The writer had been publicly challenged in the journal to say where he had resided and kept his large stock of rabbits while carrying on his experiments, which must have consumed several years, and no answer could be extracted from him.

My habits are methodical, and this has been of not a little use for my particular line of work. Lastly, I have had ample leisure from not having to earn my own bread. Even ill-health, though it has annihilated several years of my life, has saved me from the distractions of society and amusement.

Therefore, my success as a man of science, whatever this may have amounted to, has been determined, as far as I can judge, by complex and diversified mental qualities and conditions. Of these, the most important have been—the love of science—unbounded patience in long reflecting over any subject—industry in observing and collecting facts—and a fair share of invention as well as of common-sense. With such moderate abilities as I possess, it is truly surprising that I should have influenced to a considerable extent the belief of scientific men on some important points.

[1] The falseness of the published statements on which Mr. Huth relied were pointed out in a slip inserted in all the unsold copies of his book, *The Marriage of near Kin.*—F. D.

APPENDICES

BY SIR FRANCIS DARWIN

I

REMINISCENCES OF MY FATHER'S EVERYDAY LIFE

IT is my wish in the present work to give some idea of my father's everyday life. It has seemed to me that I might carry out this object in the form of a rough sketch of a day's life at Down, interspersed with such recollections as are called up by the record. Many of these recollections, which have a meaning for those who knew my father, will seem colourless or trifling to strangers. Nevertheless, I give them in the hope that they may help to preserve that impression of his personality which remains on the minds of those who knew and loved him—an impression at once so vivid and so untranslatable into words.

Of his personal appearance (in these days of multiplied photographs) it is hardly necessary to say much. He was about six feet in height, but scarcely looked so tall, as he stooped a good deal ; in later days he yielded to the stoop ; but I can remember seeing him long ago swinging back his arms to open out his chest, and holding himself upright with a jerk. He gave one the idea that he had been active rather than strong ; his shoulders were not broad for his height, though certainly not narrow. As a young man he must have had much endurance, for on one of the shore excursions from the *Beagle*, when all were suffering from want of water, he was one of the two who were better able than the rest to struggle on in search of it. As a boy he was active, and could jump a bar placed at the height of the " Adam's apple " in his neck.

He walked with a swinging action, using a stick heavily shod with iron, which he struck loudly against the ground, producing as he went round the " Sandwalk " at Down, a rhythmical click which is with all of us a very distinct remembrance. As he returned from the mid-day walk, often carrying the waterproof or cloak which had proved too hot, one could see that the swinging step was kept up by something of an effort. Indoors his step was often slow and laboured, and as he went upstairs in the afternoon he might be heard mounting the stairs with a heavy footfall, as if each step were an effort. When interested in his work he moved about quickly and easily enough, and often in the midst of dictating he went eagerly into the hall to get a pinch of snuff, leaving the study door open, and calling out the last words of his sentence as he left the room.

In spite of his activity, he had, I think, no natural grace or neatness of movement. He was awkward with his hands, and was unable to draw at all well.[1] This he always regretted, and he frequently urged the

[1] The figure in *Insectivorous Plants* representing the aggregated cell-contents was drawn by him.

paramount necessity to a young naturalist of making himself a good draughtsman.

He could dissect well under the simple microscope, but I think it was by dint of his great patience and carefulness. It was characteristic of him that he thought any little bit of skilful dissection something almost superhuman. He used to speak with admiration of the skill with which he saw Newport dissect a humble bee, getting out the nervous system with a few cuts of a pair of fine scissors. He used to consider cutting microscopic sections a great feat, and in the last year of his life, with wonderful energy, took the pains to learn to cut sections of roots and leaves. His hand was not steady enough to hold the object to be cut, and he employed a common microtome, in which the pith for holding the object was clamped, and the razor slid on a glass surface. He used to laugh at himself, and at his own skill in section-cutting, at which he would say he was " speechless with admiration." On the other hand, he must have had accuracy of eye and power of co-ordinating his movements, since he was a good shot with a gun as a young man, and as a boy was skilful in throwing. He once killed a hare sitting in the flower-garden at Shrewsbury by throwing a marble at it, and, as a man, he killed a cross-beak with a stone. He was so unhappy at having uselessly killed the cross-beak that he did not mention it for years, and then explained that he should never have thrown at it if he had not felt sure that his old skill had gone from him.

His beard was full and almost untrimmed, the hair being grey and white, fine rather than coarse, and wavy or frizzled. His moustache was somewhat disfigured by being cut short and square across. He became very bald, having only a fringe of dark hair behind.

His face was ruddy in colour, and this perhaps made people think him less of an invalid than he was. He wrote to Sir Joseph Hooker (June 13, 1849), " Every one tells me that I look quite blooming and beautiful ; and most think I am shamming, but you have never been one of those." And it must be remembered that at this time he was miserably ill, far worse than in later years. His eyes were bluish grey under deep overhanging brows, with thick, bushy projecting eyebrows. His high forehead was deeply wrinkled, but otherwise his face was not much marked or lined. His expression showed no signs of the continual discomfort he suffered.

When he was excited with pleasant talk his whole manner was wonderfully bright and animated, and his face shared to the full in the general animation. His laugh was a free and sounding peal, like that of a man who gives himself sympathetically and with enjoyment to the person and the thing which have amused him. He often used some sort of gesture with his laugh, lifting up his hands or bringing one down with a slap. I think, generally speaking, he was given to gesture, and often used his hands in explaining anything (*e.g.* the fertilisation of a flower) in a way that seemed rather an aid to himself than to the listener. He did this on occasions when most people would illustrate their explanations by means of a rough pencil sketch.

He wore dark clothes, of a loose and easy fit. Of late years he gave up the tall hat even in London, and wore a soft black one in winter, and a big straw hat in summer. His usual out-of-doors dress was the short cloak in which Elliott and Fry's photograph[1] represents him, leaning against the pillar of the verandah. Two peculiarities of his indoor dress were that he almost always wore a shawl over his shoulders, and that he had great loose cloth boots lined with fur which he could slip on over his indoor shoes.

He rose early, and took a short turn before breakfast, a habit which began when he went for the first time to a water-cure establishment, and was preserved till almost the end of his life. I used, as a little boy, to like going out with him, and I have a vague sense of the red of the winter sunrise, and a recollection of the pleasant companionship, and a certain honour and glory in it. He used to delight me as a boy by telling me how, in still earlier walks, on dark winter mornings, he had once or twice met foxes trotting home at the dawning.

After breakfasting alone about 7.45, he went to work at once, considering the $1\frac{1}{2}$ hour between 8 and 9.30 one of his best working times. At 9.30 he came in to the drawing-room for his letters—rejoicing if the post was a light one and being sometimes much worried if it was not. He would then hear any family letters read aloud as he lay on the sofa.

The reading aloud, which also included part of a novel, lasted till about half-past ten, when he went back to work till twelve or a quarter past. By this time he considered his day's work over, and would often say, in a satisfied voice, " *I've* done a good day's work." He then went out of doors whether it was wet or fine ; Polly, his white terrier, went with him in fair weather, but in rain she refused or might be seen hesitating in the verandah, with a mixed expression of disgust and shame at her own want of courage ; generally, however, her conscience carried the day, and as soon as he was evidently gone she could not bear to stay behind.

My father was always fond of dogs, and as a young man had the power of stealing away the affections of his sister's pets : at Cambridge, he won the love of his cousin W. D. Fox's dog, and this may perhaps have been the little beast which used to creep down inside his bed and sleep at the foot every night. My father had a surly dog, who was devoted to him, but unfriendly to every one else, and when he came back from the *Beagle* voyage, the dog remembered him, but in a curious way, which my father was fond of telling. He went into the yard and shouted in his old manner ; the dog rushed out and set off with him on his walk, showing no more emotion or excitement than if the same thing had happened the day before, instead of five years ago. This story is made use of in the *Descent of Man*, 2nd Edit. p. 74.

In my memory there were only two dogs which had much connection with my father. One was a large black and white half-bred retriever, called Bob, to which we, as children, were much devoted. He was the dog of whom the story of the " hot-house face " is told in the *Expression of the Emotions*.

But the dog most closely associated with my father was the above-mentioned Polly, a rough, white fox-terrier. She was a sharp-witted, affectionate dog ; when her master was going away on a journey, she always discovered the fact by the signs of packing going on in the study, and became low-spirited accordingly. She began, too, to be excited by seeing the study prepared for his return home. She was a cunning little creature, and used to tremble or put on an air of misery when my father passed, while she was waiting for dinner, just as if she knew that he would say (as he did often say) that " she was famishing." My father used to make her catch biscuits off her nose, and had an affectionate and mock-solemn way of explaining to her before-hand that she must " be a very good girl." She had a mark on her back where she had been burnt, and where the hair had re-grown red instead of white, and my father used to commend her for this tuft of hair as being in accordance with his theory of pangenesis ; her father had been a red bull-terrier, thus the red hair appearing after the burn showed the presence of latent red gemmules. He was delightfully tender to Polly, and never showed any impatience at the attentions she required, such as to be let in at the door, or out at the verandah window, to bark at " naughty people," a self-imposed duty she much enjoyed. She died, or rather had to be killed, a few days after his death.

My father's mid-day walk generally began by a call at the greenhouse, where he looked at any germinating seeds or experimental plants which required a casual examination, but he hardly ever did any serious observing at this time. Then he went on for his constitutional—either round the " Sand-walk," or outside his own grounds in the immediate neighbourhood of the house. The " Sand-walk " was a narrow strip of land $1\frac{1}{2}$ acre in extent, with a gravel-walk round it. On one side of it was a broad old shaw with fair-sized oaks in it, which made a sheltered shady walk ; the other side was separated from a neighbouring grass field by a low quickset hedge, over which you could look at what view there was, a quiet little valley losing itself in the upland country towards the edge of the Westerham hill, with hazel coppice and larch plantation, the remnants of what was once a large wood, stretching away to the Westerham high road. I have heard my father say that the charm of this simple little valley was a decided factor in his choice of a home.

The Sand-walk was planted by my father with a variety of trees, such as hazel, alder, lime, hornbeam, birch, privet, and dogwood, and with a long line of hollies all down the exposed side. In earlier times he took a certain number of turns every day, and used to count them by means of a heap of flints, one of which he kicked out on the path each time he passed. Of late years I think he did not keep to any fixed number of turns, but took as many as he felt strength for. The Sand-walk was our play-ground as children, and here we continually saw my father as he walked round. He liked to see what we were doing, and was ever ready to sympathise in any fun that was going on. It is curious to think how, with regard to the Sand-walk in connection with my father, my earliest recollections coincide with my latest ; it shows the unvarying character of his habits.

Sometimes when alone he stood still or walked stealthily to observe birds or beasts. It was on one of these occasions that some young squirrels ran up his back and legs, while their mother barked at them in an agony from the tree. He always found birds' nests even up to the last years of his life, and we, as children, considered that he had a special genius in this direction. In his quiet prowls he came across the less common birds, but I fancy he used to conceal it from me as a little boy, because he observed the agony of mind which I endured at not having seen the siskin or goldfinch, or some other of the less common birds. He used to tell us how, when he was creeping noiselessly along in the " Big-Woods," he came upon a fox asleep in the daytime, which was so much astonished that it took a good stare at him before it ran off. A Spitz dog which accompanied him showed no sign of excitement at the fox, and he used to end the story by wondering how the dog could have been so faint-hearted.

Another favourite place was " Orchis Bank," above the quiet Cudham valley, where fly- and musk-orchis grew among the junipers, and Cephalanthera and Neottia under the beech boughs ; the little wood " Hangrove," just above this, he was also fond of, and here I remember his collecting grasses, when he took a fancy to make out the names of all the common kinds. He was fond of quoting the saying of one of his little boys, who, having found a grass that his father had not seen before, had it laid by his own plate during dinner, remarking, " I are an extraordinary grass-finder ! "

My father much enjoyed wandering idly in the garden with my mother or some of his children, or making one of a party, sitting on a bench on the lawn ; he generally sat, however, on the grass, and I remember him often lying under one of the big lime-trees, with his head on the green mound at its foot. In dry summer weather, when we often sat out, the fly-wheel of the well was commonly heard spinning round, and so•the sound became associated with those pleasant days. He used to like to watch us playing at lawn-tennis, and often knocked up a stray ball for us with the curved handle of his stick.

Though he took no personal share in the management of the garden, he had great delight in the beauty of flowers—for instance, in the mass of Azaleas which generally stood in the drawing-room. I think he sometimes fused together his admiration of the structure of a flower and of its intrinsic beauty ; for instance in the case of the big pendulous pink and white flowers of Diclytra. In the same way he had an affection, half-artistic, half-botanical, for the little blue Lobelia. In admiring flowers, he would often laugh at the dingy high-art colours, and contrast them with the bright tints of nature. I used to like to hear him admire the beauty of a flower ; it was a kind of gratitude to the flower itself, and a personal love for its delicate form and colour. I seem to remember him gently touching a flower he delighted in ; it was the same simple admiration that a child might have.

He could not help personifying natural things. This feeling came out in abuse as well as in praise— *e.g.* of some seedlings—" The little beggars are doing just what I don't want them to." He would speak in a half-provoked, half-admiring way of the ingenuity of the leaf of a sensitive plant in screwing itself out of a basin of water in which he had tried to fix it. One might see the same spirit in his way of speaking of Sundew, earthworms, &c.[1]

Within my memory, his only outdoor recreation, besides walking, was riding ; this was taken up at the recommendation of Dr. Bence Jones, and we had the luck to find for him the easiest and quietest cob in the world, named " Tommy." He enjoyed these rides extremely, and devised a series of short rounds which brought him home in time for lunch. Our country is good for this purpose, owing to the number of small valleys which give a variety to what in a flat country would be a dull loop of road. I think he felt surprised at himself, when he remembered how bold a rider he had been, and how utterly old age and bad health had taken away his nerve. He would say that riding prevented him thinking much more effectually than walking—that having to attend to the horse gave him occupation sufficient to prevent any really hard thinking. And the change of scene which it gave him was good for spirits and health.

If I go beyond my own experience, and recall what I have heard him say of his love for sport, &c., I can think of a good deal, but much of it would be a repetition of what is contained in his *Recollections*. He was fond of his gun as quite a boy, and became a good shot ; he used to tell how in South America he killed twenty-three snipe in twenty-four shots. In telling the story he was careful to add that

---

[1] Cf. Leslie Stephen's *Swift*, 1882, p. 200, where Swift's inspection of the manners and customs of servants are compared to my father's observations on worms, " The difference is," says Mr. Stephen, " that Darwin had none but kindly feelings for worms."

he thought they were not quite so wild as English snipe.

Luncheon at Down came after his mid-day walk ; and here I may say a word or two about his meals generally. He had a boy-like love of sweets, unluckily for himself, since he was constantly forbidden to take them. He was not particularly successful in keeping the " vows," as he called them, which he made against eating sweets, and never considered them binding unless he made them aloud.

He drank very little wine, but enjoyed and was revived by the little he did drink. He had a horror of drinking, and constantly warned his boys that any one might be led into drinking too much. I remember, in my innocence as a small boy, asking him if he had been ever tipsy ; and he answered very gravely that he was ashamed to say he had once drunk too much at Cambridge. I was much impressed, so that I know now the place where the question was asked.

After his lunch he read the newspaper, lying on the sofa in the drawing-room. I think the paper was the only non-scientific matter which he read to himself. Everything else, novels, travels, history, was read aloud to him. He took so wide an interest in life, that there was much to occupy him in newspapers, though he laughed at the wordiness of the debates, reading them, I think, only in abstract. His interest in politics was considerable, but his opinion on these matters was formed rather by the way than with any serious amount of thought.

After he had read his paper, came his time for writing letters. These, as well as the MS. of his books, were written by him as he sat in a huge horse-hair chair by the fire, his paper supported on a board resting on the arms of the chair. When he had many or long letters to write, he would dictate them from a rough copy; these rough copies were written on the backs of manuscript or of proof-sheets, and were almost illegible, sometimes even to himself. He made a rule of keeping all letters that he received; this was a habit which he learnt from his father, and which he said had been of great use to him.

Many letters were addressed to him by foolish, unscrupulous people, and all of these received replies. He used to say that if he did not answer them, he had it on his conscience afterwards, and no doubt it was in great measure the courtesy with which he answered every one which produced the widespread sense of his kindness of nature which was so evident on his death.

He was considerate to his correspondents in other and lesser things—for instance, when dictating a letter to a foreigner, he hardly ever failed to say to me, " You'd better try and write well, as it's to a foreigner." His letters were generally written on the assumption that they would be carelessly read; thus, when he was dictating, he was careful to tell me to make an important clause begin with an obvious paragraph, " to catch his eye," as he often said. How much he thought of the trouble he gave others by asking questions, will be well enough shown by his letters.

He had a printed form to be used in replying to troublesome correspondents, but he hardly ever used it; I suppose he never found an occasion that seemed exactly suitable. I remember an occasion on which it might have been used with advantage. He received a letter from a stranger stating that the writer had undertaken to uphold Evolution at a debating society, and that being a busy young man, without time for reading, he wished to have a sketch of my father's views. Even this wonderful young man got a civil answer, though I think he did not get much material for his speech. His rule was to thank the donors of books, but not of pamphlets. He sometimes expressed surprise that so few thanked him for his books which he gave away liberally; the letters that he did receive gave him much pleasure, because he habitually formed so humble an estimate of the value of all his works, that he was genuinely surprised at the interest which they excited.

In money and business matters he was remarkably careful and exact. He kept accounts with great care, classifying them, and balancing at the end of the year like a merchant. I remember the quick way in which he would reach out for his account-book to enter each cheque paid, as though he were in a hurry to get it entered before he had forgotten it. His father must have allowed him to believe that he would be poorer than he really was, for some of the difficulty experienced over finding a house in the country must have arisen from the modest sum he felt prepared to give. Yet he knew, of course, that he would be in easy circumstances, for in his *Recollections* he mentions this as one of the reasons for his not having worked at medicine with so much zeal as he would have done if he had been obliged to gain his living.

He had a pet economy in paper, but it was rather

a hobby than a real economy.   All the blank sheets of letters received were kept in a portfolio to be used in making notes ; it was his respect for paper that made him write so much on the backs of his old MS., and in this way, unfortunately, he destroyed large parts of the original MS. of his books.   His feeling about paper extended to waste paper, and he objected, half in fun, to the habit of throwing a spill into the fire after it had been used for lighting a candle.

He had a great respect for pure business capacity, and often spoke with admiration of a relative who had doubled his fortune.   And of himself would often say in fun that what he really *was* proud of was the money he had saved.   He also felt satisfaction in the money he made by his books.   His anxiety to save came in great measure from his fears that his children would not have health enough to earn their own livings, a foreboding which fairly haunted him for many years.   And I have a dim recollection of his saying, " Thank God, you'll have bread and cheese," when I was so young that I was inclined to take it literally.

When letters were finished, about three in the afternoon, he rested in his bedroom, lying on the sofa, smoking a cigarette, and listening to a novel or other book not scientific.   He only smoked when resting, whereas snuff was a stimulant, and was taken during working hours.   He took snuff for many years of his life, having learnt the habit at Edinburgh as a student.   He had a nice silver snuff-box given him by Mrs. Wedgwood, of Maer, which he valued much— but he rarely carried it, because it tempted him to take too many pinches.   In one of his early letters he speaks of having given up snuff for a month, and describes himself as feeling "most lethargic, stupid, and melancholy." Our former neighbour and clergyman, Mr. Brodie Innes, tells me that at one time my father made a resolve not to take snuff, except away from home, "a most satisfactory arrangement for me," he adds, "as I kept a box in my study, to which there was access from the garden without summoning servants, and I had more frequently, than might have been otherwise the case, the privilege of a few minutes' conversation with my dear friend." He generally took snuff from a jar on the hall-table, because having to go this distance for a pinch was a slight check ; the clink of the lid of the snuff-jar was a very familiar sound. Sometimes when he was in the drawing-room, it would occur to him that the study fire must be burning low, and when one of us offered to see after it, it would turn out that he also wished to get a pinch of snuff.

Smoking he only took to permanently of late years, though on his Pampas rides he learned to smoke with the Gauchos, and I have heard him speak of the great comfort of a cup of *maté* and a cigarette when he halted after a long ride and was unable to get food for some time.

He came down at four o'clock to dress for his walk, and he was so regular that one might be quite certain it was within a few minutes of four when his descending steps were heard.

From about half-past four to half-past five he worked ; then he came to the drawing-room, and was idle till it was time (about six) to go up for another rest with novel-reading and a cigarette.

Latterly he gave up late dinner, and had a simple tea at half-past seven (while we had dinner), with an egg or a small piece of meat. After dinner he never stayed in the room, and used to apologise by saying he was an old woman who must be allowed to leave with the ladies. This was one of the many signs and results of his constant weakness and ill-health. Half an hour more or less conversation would make to him the difference of a sleepless night and of the loss perhaps of half the next day's work.

After dinner he played backgammon with my mother, two games being played every night. For many years a score of the games which each won was kept, and in this score he took the greatest interest. He became extremely animated over these games, bitterly lamenting his bad luck and exploding with exaggerated mock-anger at my mother's good fortune.

After playing backgammon he read some scientific book to himself, either in the drawing-room, or, if much talking was going on, in the study.

In the evening—that is, after he had read as much as his strength would allow, and before the reading aloud began—he would often lie on the sofa and listen to my mother playing the piano. He had not a good ear, yet in spite of this he had a true love of fine music. He used to lament that his enjoyment of music had become dulled with age, yet within my recollection his love of a good tune was strong. I never heard him hum more than one tune, the Welsh song "Ar hyd y nos," which he went through correctly; he used also, I believe, to hum a little Otaheitan song. From his want of ear he was unable to recognise a tune when he heard it again, but he remained constant to what he liked, and would often say, when an old favourite was played, " That's a fine thing ; what is it ? " He liked especially parts of Beethoven's symphonies and bits of Handel. He was sensitive to differences in style, and enjoyed the late Mrs. Vernon Lushington's playing intensely, and in June 1881, when Hans Richter paid a visit at Down, he was roused to strong enthusiasm by his magnificent performance on the piano. He enjoyed good singing, and was moved almost to tears by grand or pathetic songs. His niece Lady Farrer's singing of Sullivan's " Will he come " was a never-failing enjoyment to him. He was humble in the extreme about his own taste, and correspondingly pleased when he found that others agreed with him.

He became much tired in the evenings, especially of late years, and left the drawing-room about ten, going to bed at half-past ten. His nights were generally bad, and he often lay awake or sat up in bed for hours, suffering much discomfort. He was troubled at night by the activity of his thoughts, and would become exhausted by his mind working at some problem which he would willingly have dismissed. At night, too, anything which had vexed or troubled him in the day would haunt him, and I think it was then that he suffered if he had not answered some troublesome correspondent.

The regular readings, which I have mentioned, continued for so many years, enabled him to get through a great deal of the lighter kinds of literature. He was extremely fond of novels, and I remember well the way in which he would anticipate the pleasure of having a novel read to him as he lay down or lighted his cigarette. He took a vivid interest both in plot and characters, and would on no account know beforehand how a story finished ; he considered looking at the end of a novel as a feminine vice. He could not enjoy any story with a tragical end ; for this reason he did not keenly appreciate George Eliot, though he often spoke warmly in praise of *Silas Marner*. Walter Scott, Miss Austen, and Mrs. Gaskell were read and re-read till they could be read no more. He had two or three books in hand at the same time—a novel and perhaps a biography and a book of travels. He did not often read out-of-the-way or old standard books, but generally kept to the books of the day obtained from a circulating library.

His literary tastes and opinions were not on a level with the rest of his mind. He himself, though he was clear as to what he thought good, considered that in matters of literary tastes he was quite outside the pale, and often spoke of what those within it liked or disliked, as if they formed a class to which he had no claim to belong.

In all matters of art he was inclined to laugh at professed critics and say that their opinions were formed by fashion. Thus in painting, he would say how in his day every one admired masters who are now neglected. His love of pictures as a young man is almost a proof that he must have had an appreciation of a portrait as a work of art, not as a likeness. Yet he often talked laughingly of the small worth of portraits, and said that a photograph was worth any number of pictures, as if he were blind to the artistic quality in a painted portrait. But this was generally said in his attempts to persuade us to give up the idea of having his portrait painted, an operation very irksome to him.

This way of looking at himself as an ignoramus in all matters of art, was strengthened by the absence of pretence, which was part of his character. With regard to questions of taste, as well as to more serious things, he had the courage of his opinions. I remember, however, an instance that sounds like a contradiction to this : when he was looking at the Turners in Mr. Ruskin's bedroom, he did not confess, as he did afterwards, that he could make out absolutely nothing of what Mr. Ruskin saw in them. But this little pretence was not for his own sake, but for the sake of courtesy to his host. He was pleased and amused when subsequently Mr. Ruskin brought him some photographs of pictures (I think Vandyke portraits), and courteously seemed to value my father's opinion about them.

Much of his scientific reading was in German, and this was a serious labour to him ; in reading a book after him, I was often struck at seeing, from the pencil-marks made each day where he left off, how little he could read at a time. He used to call German the " Verdammte," pronounced as if in English. He was especially indignant with Germans, because he was convinced that they could write simply if they chose, and often praised Professor Hildebrand of Freiburg for writing German which was as clear as French. He sometimes gave a German sentence to a friend, a patriotic German lady, and used to laugh at her if she did not translate it fluently. He himself learnt German simply by hammering away with a dictionary ; he would say that his only way was to read a sentence a great many times over, and at last the meaning occurred to him. When he began German long ago, he boasted of the fact (as he used to tell) to Sir J. Hooker, who replied, " Ah, my dear fellow, that's nothing ; I've begun it many times."

In spite of his want of grammar, he managed to get on wonderfully with German, and the sentences that he failed to make out were generally difficult ones. He never attempted to speak German correctly, but pronounced the words as though they were English ; and this made it not a little difficult to help him, when he read out a German sentence and asked for a translation. He certainly had a bad ear for vocal sounds, so that he found it impossible to perceive small differences in pronunciation.

His wide interest in branches of science that were not specially his own was remarkable. In the biological sciences his doctrines make themselves felt so widely that there was something interesting to him in most departments. He read a good deal of many quite special works, and large parts of text books, such as Huxley's *Invertebrate Anatomy*, or such a book as Balfour's *Embryology*, where the detail, at any rate, was not specially in his own line. And in the case of elaborate books of the monograph type, though he did not make a study of them, yet he felt the strongest admiration for them.

In the non-biological sciences he felt keen sympathy with work of which he could not really judge. For instance, he used to read nearly the whole of *Nature*, though so much of it deals with mathematics and physics. I have often heard him say that he got a kind of satisfaction in reading articles which (according to himself) he could not understand. I wish I could reproduce the manner in which he would laugh at himself for it.

It was remarkable, too, how he kept up his interest in subjects at which he had formerly worked. This was strikingly the case with geology. In one of his letters to Mr. Judd he begs him to pay him a visit, saying that since Lyell's death he hardly ever gets a geological talk. His observations, made only a few years before his death, on the upright pebbles in the drift at Southampton, and discussed in a letter to Sir A. Geikie, afford another instance. Again, in his letters to Dr. Dohrn, he shows how his interest in barnacles remained alive. I think it was all due to the vitality and persistence of his mind—a quality I have heard him speak of as if he felt that he was strongly gifted in that respect. Not that he used any such phrases as these about himself, but he would say that he had the power of keeping a subject or question more or less before him for a great many years. The extent to which he possessed this power appears when we consider the number of different problems which he solved, and the early period at which some of them began to occupy him.

It was a sure sign that he was not well when he was idle at any times other than his regular resting hours ; for, as long as he remained moderately well, there was no break in the regularity of his life. Week-days and Sundays passed by alike, each with their stated intervals of work and rest. It is almost impossible, except for those who watched his daily life, to realise how essential to his well-being was the regular routine that I have sketched : and with what pain and difficulty anything beyond it was attempted. Any public appearance, even of the most modest kind, was an effort to him. In 1871 he went to the little village church for the wedding of his elder daughter, but he could hardly bear the fatigue of being present through the short service. The same may be said of the few other occasions on which he was present at similar ceremonies.

I remember him many years ago at a christening ; a memory which has remained with me, because to us children his being at church was an extraordinary occurrence. I remember his look most distinctly at his brother Erasmus's funeral, as he stood in the scattering of snow, wrapped in a long black funeral cloak, with a grave look of sad reverie.

When, after an absence of many years, he attended a meeting of the Linnean Society, it was felt to be, and was in fact, a serious undertaking ; one not to be determined on without much sinking of heart, and hardly to be carried into effect without paying a penalty of subsequent suffering. In the same way a breakfast-party at Sir James Paget's, with some of the distinguished visitors to the Medical Congress (1881), was to him a severe exertion.

The early morning was the only time at which he could make any effort of the kind, with comparative impunity. Thus it came about that the visits he paid to his scientific friends in London were by preference made as early as ten in the morning. For the same reason he started on his journeys by the earliest possible train, and used to arrive at the houses of relatives in London when they were beginning their day.

He kept an accurate journal of the days on which he worked and those on which his ill health prevented him from working, so that it would be possible to tell how many were idle days in any given year. In this journal—a little yellow Letts's Diary, which lay open on his mantel-piece, piled on the diaries of previous years—he also entered the day on which he started for a holiday and that of his return.

The most frequent holidays were visits of a week to London, either to his brother's house (6 Queen Anne Street), or to his daughter's (4 Bryanston Street). He was generally persuaded by my mother to take these short holidays, when it became clear from the frequency of "bad days," or from the swimming of his head, that he was being overworked. He went unwillingly, and tried to drive hard bargains, stipulating, for instance, that he should come home in five days instead of six. The discomfort of a journey to him was, at least latterly, chiefly in the anticipation, and in the miserable sinking feeling from which he suffered immediately before the start ; even a fairly long journey, such as that to Coniston, tired him wonderfully little, considering how much an invalid he was ; and he certainly enjoyed it in an almost boyish way, and to a curious degree.

Although, as he has said, some of his æsthetic tastes had suffered a gradual decay, his love of scenery remained fresh and strong. Every walk at Coniston was a fresh delight, and he was never tired of praising the beauty of the broken hilly country at the head of the lake.

Besides these longer holidays, there were shorter visits to various relatives—to his brother-in-law's house, close to Leith Hill, and to his son near Southampton. He always particularly enjoyed rambling over rough open country, such as the commons near Leith Hill and Southampton, the heath-covered wastes of Ashdown Forest, or the delightful " Rough " near the house of his friend Sir Thomas Farrer. He never was quite idle even on these holidays, and found things to observe. At Hartfield he watched Drosera catching insects, &c. ; at Torquay he observed the fertilisation of an orchid (*Spiranthes*), and also made out the relations of the sexes in Thyme.

He rejoiced at his return home after his holidays, and greatly enjoyed the welcome he got from his dog Polly, who would get wild with excitement, panting, squeaking, rushing round the room, and jumping on and off the chairs ; and he used to stoop down, pressing her face to his, letting her lick him, and speaking to her with a peculiarly tender, caressing voice.

My father had the power of giving to these summer holidays a charm which was strongly felt by all his family. The pressure of his work at home kept him at the utmost stretch of his powers of endurance, and when released from it, he entered on a holiday with a youthfulness of enjoyment that made his companionship delightful ; we felt that we saw more of him in a week's holiday than in a month at home.

Besides the holidays which I have mentioned, there were his visits to water-cure establishments. In

1849, when very ill, suffering from constant sickness, he was urged by a friend to try the water-cure, and at last agreed to go to Dr. Gully's establishment at Malvern. His letters to Mr. Fox show how much good the treatment did him ; he seems to have thought that he had found a cure for his troubles, but, like all other remedies, it had only a transient effect on him. However, he found it, at first, so good for him, that when he came home he built himself a douche-bath, and the butler learnt to be his bathman.

He was, too, a frequent patient at Dr. Lane's water-cure establishment, Moor Park, near Aldershot, visits to which he always looked back with pleasure.

Some idea of his relation to his family and his friends may be gathered from what has gone before ; it would be impossible to attempt a complete account of these relationships, but a slightly fuller outline may not be out of place. Of his married life I cannot speak, save in the briefest manner. In his relationship towards my mother, his tender and sympathetic nature was shown in its most beautiful aspect. In her presence he found his happiness, and through her, his life—which might have been over-shadowed by gloom—became one of content and quiet gladness.

The *Expression of the Emotions* shows how closely he watched his children ; it was characteristic of him that (as I have heard him tell), although he was so anxious to observe accurately the expression of a crying child, his sympathy with the grief spoiled his observation. His note-book, in which are recorded sayings of his young children, shows his pleasure in them. He seemed to retain a sort of regretful memory of the childhoods which had faded away, and thus he wrote in his *Recollections* :—" When you were very young it was my delight to play with you all, and I think with a sigh that such days can never return."

I quote, as showing the tenderness of his nature, some sentences from an account of his little daughter Annie, written a few days after her death :—

" Our poor child, Annie, was born in Gower Street, on March 2, 1841, and expired at Malvern at mid-day on the 23rd of April, 1851.

" I write these few pages, as I think in after years, if we live, the impressions now put down will recall more vividly her chief characteristics. From what-ever point I look back at her, the main feature in her disposition which at once rises before me, is her buoyant joyousness, tempered by two other charac-teristics, namely, her sensitiveness, which might easily have been overlooked by a stranger, and her strong affection. Her joyousness and animal spirits radiated from her whole countenance, and rendered every movement elastic and full of life and vigour. It was delightful and cheerful to behold her. Her dear face now rises before me, as she used sometimes to come running downstairs with a stolen pinch of snuff for me, her whole form radiant with the pleasure of giving pleasure. Even when playing with her cousins, when her joyousness almost passed into boisterousness, a single glance of my eye, not of dis-pleasure (for I thank God I hardly ever cast one on her), but of want of sympathy, would for some minutes alter her whole countenance.

" The other point in her character, which made her joyousness and spirits so delightful, was her strong affection, which was of a most clinging, fondling nature. When quite a baby, this showed itself in never being easy without touching her mother, when in bed with her ; and quite lately she would, when poorly, fondle for any length of time one of her mother's arms. When very unwell, her mother lying down beside her, seemed to soothe her in a manner quite different from what it would have done to any of our other children. So, again, she would at almost any time spend half an hour in arranging my hair, ' making it,' as she called it, ' beautiful,' or in smoothing, the poor dear darling, my collar or cuffs—in short, in fondling me.

" Besides her joyousness thus tempered, she was in her manners remarkably cordial, frank, open, straightforward, natural, and without any shade of reserve. Her whole mind was pure and transparent. One felt one knew her thoroughly and could trust her. I always thought, that come what might, we should have had, in our old age, at least one loving soul, which nothing could have changed. All her movements were vigorous, active, and usually grace-ful. When going round the Sand-walk with me, although I walked fast, yet she often used to go before, pirouetting in the most elegant way, her dear face bright all the time with the sweetest smiles. Occasionally she had a pretty coquettish manner towards me, the memory of which is charming. She often used exaggerated language, and when I quizzed her by exaggerating what she had said, how clearly can I now see the little toss of the head, and exclamation of ' Oh, papa, what a shame of you ! ' In the last short illness, her conduct in simple truth was angelic. She never once complained ; never became fretful ; was ever considerate of others, and was thankful in the most gentle, pathetic manner for everything done for her. When so exhausted that she could hardly speak, she praised everything that was given her, and said some tea 'was beautifully good.' When I gave her some water, she said, ' I quite thank you ; ' and these, I believe, were the last precious words ever addressed by her dear lips to me.

" We have lost the joy of the household, and the solace of our old age. She must have known how we loved her. Oh, that she could now know how deeply, how tenderly, we. do still and shall ever love her dear joyous face ! Blessings on her ! [1]

" April 30, 1851."

We, his children, all took especial pleasure in the games he played at with us, and in his stories, which, partly on account of their rarity, were considered specially delightful.

The way he brought us up is shown by a little story about my brother Leonard, which my father was fond of telling. He came into the drawing-room and found Leonard dancing about on the sofa, to the peril of the springs, and said, " Oh, Lenny, Lenny, that's against all rules," and received for answer, " Then I think you'd better go out of the room." I do not believe he ever spoke an angry

[1] The words, " A good and dear child," form the descriptive part of the inscription on her gravestone. See the *Athenæum*, Nov. 26, 1887.

word to any of his children in his life ; but I am certain that it never entered our heads to disobey him. I well remember one occasion when my father reproved me for a piece of carelessness ; and I can still recall the feeling of depression which came over me, and the care which he took to disperse it by speaking to me soon afterwards with especial kindness. He kept up his delightful, affectionate manner towards us all his life. I sometimes wonder that he could do so, with such an undemonstrative race as we are ; but I hope he knew how much we delighted in his loving words and manner. He allowed his grown-up children to laugh with and at him, and was generally speaking on terms of perfect equality with us.

He was always full of interest about each one's plans or successes. We used to laugh at him, and say he would not believe in his sons, because, for instance, he would be a little doubtful about their taking some bit of work for which he did not feel sure that they had knowledge enough. On the other hand, he was only too much inclined to take a favourable view of our work. When I thought he had set too high a value on anything that I had done, he used to be indignant and inclined to explode in mock anger. His doubts were part of his humility concerning what was in any way connected with himself ; his too favourable view of our work was due to his sympathetic nature, which made him lenient to every one.

He kept up towards his children his delightful manner of expressing his thanks ; and I never wrote a letter, or read a page aloud to him, without receiving a few kind words of recognition. His love and goodness towards his little grandson Bernard were great ; and he often spoke of the pleasure it was to him to see " his little face opposite to him " at luncheon. He and Bernard used to compare their tastes ; *e.g.*, in liking brown sugar better than white, &c. ; the result being, " We always agree, don't we ? "

My sister writes :—

" My first remembrances of my father are of the delights of his playing with us. He was passionately attached to his own children, although he was not an indiscriminate child-lover. To all of us he was the most delightful play-fellow, and the most perfect sympathiser. Indeed it is impossible adequately to describe how delightful a relation his was to his family, whether as children or in their later life.

" It is a proof of the terms on which we were, and also of how much he was valued as a play-fellow, that one of his sons when about four years old tried to bribe him with sixpence to come and play in working hours.

" He must have been the most patient and delightful of nurses. I remember the haven of peace and comfort it seemed to me when I was unwell, to be tucked up on the study sofa, idly considering the old geological map hung on the wall. This must have been in his working hours, for I always picture him sitting in the horse hair arm chair by the corner of the fire.

" Another mark of his unbounded patience was the way in which we were suffered to make raids into the study when we had an absolute need of sticking plaster, string, pins, scissors, stamps, foot rule, or hammer. These and other such necessaries were always to be found in the study, and it was the only place where this was a certainty. We used to feel it wrong to go in during work time ; still, when the necessity was great, we did so. I remember his patient look when he said once, ' Don't you think you could not come in again, I have been interrupted very often.' We used to dread going in for sticking plaster, because he disliked to see that we had cut ourselves, both for our sakes and on account of his acute sensitiveness to the sight of blood. I well remember lurking about the passage till he was safe away, and then stealing in for the plaster.

" Life seems to me, as I look back upon it, to have been very regular in those early days, and except relations (and a few intimate friends), I do not think any one came to the house. After lessons, we were always free to go where we would, and that was chiefly in the drawing-room and about the garden, so that we were very much with both my father and mother. We used to think it most delightful when he told us any stories about the *Beagle*, or about early Shrewsbury days—little bits about school life and his boyish tastes.

" He cared for all our pursuits and interests, and lived our lives with us in a way that very few fathers do. But I am certain that none of us felt that this intimacy interfered the least with our respect and obedience. Whatever he said was absolute truth and law to us. He always put his whole mind into answering any of our questions. One trifling instance makes me feel how he cared for what we cared for.

He had no special taste for cats, but yet he knew and remembered the individualities of my many cats, and would talk about the habits and characters of the more remarkable ones years after they had died.

" Another characteristic of his treatment of his children was his respect for their liberty, and for their personality. Even as quite a little girl, I remember rejoicing in this sense of freedom. Our father and mother would not even wish to know what we were doing or thinking unless we wished to tell. He always made us feel that we were each of us creatures whose opinions and thoughts were valuable to him, so that whatever there was best in us came out in the sunshine of his presence.

" I do not think his exaggerated sense of our good qualities, intellectual or moral, made us conceited, as might perhaps have been expected, but rather more humble and grateful to him. The reason being no doubt that the influence of his character, of his sincerity and greatness of nature, had a much deeper and more lasting effect than any small exaltation which his praises or admiration may have caused to our vanity." [1]

As head of a household he was much loved and respected ; he always spoke to servants with politeness, using the expression, " would you be so good," in asking for anything. He was hardly ever angry with his servants ; it shows how seldom this occurred,

[1] Some pleasant recollections of my father's life at Down, written by our friend and former neighbour, Mrs. Wallis Nash, have been published in the *Overland Monthly* (San Francisco), October 1890.

that when, as a small boy, I overheard a servant being scolded, and my father speaking angrily, it impressed me as an appalling circumstance, and I remember running upstairs out of a general sense of awe. He did not trouble himself about the management of the garden, cows, &c. He considered the horses so little his concern, that he used to ask doubtfully whether he might have a horse and cart to send to Keston for Sundew, or to the Westerham nurseries for plants, or the like.

As a host my father had a peculiar charm : the presence of visitors excited him, and made him appear to his best advantage. At Shrewsbury, he used to say, it was his father's wish that the guests should be attended to constantly, and in one of the letters to Fox he speaks of the impossibility of writing a letter while the house was full of company. I think he always felt uneasy at not doing more for the entertainment of his guests, but the result was successful ; and, to make up for any loss, there was the gain that the guests felt perfectly free to do as they liked. The most usual visitors were those who stayed from Saturday till Monday ; those who remained longer were generally relatives, and were considered to be rather more my mother's affair than his.

Besides these visitors, there were foreigners and other strangers, who came down for luncheon and went away in the afternoon. He used conscientiously to represent to them the enormous distance of Down from London, and the labour it would be to come there, unconsciously taking for granted that they would find the journey as toilsome as he did himself.

If, however, they were not deterred, he used to arrange their journeys for them, telling them when to come, and practically when to go. It was pleasant to see the way in which he shook hands with a guest who was being welcomed for the first time; his hand used to shoot out in a way that gave one the feeling that it was hastening to meet the guest's hands. With old friends his hand came down with a hearty swing into the other hand in a way I always had satisfaction in seeing. His good-bye was chiefly characterised by the pleasant way in which he thanked his guests, as he stood at the hall-door, for having come to see him.

These luncheons were successful entertainments, there was no drag or flagging about them, my father was bright and excited throughout the whole visit. Professor De Candolle has described a visit to Down, in his admirable and sympathetic sketch of my father.[1] He speaks of his manner as resembling that of a " savant " of Oxford or Cambridge. This does not strike me as quite a good comparison ; in his ease and naturalness there was more of the manner of some soldiers ; a manner arising from total absence of pretence or affectation. It was this absence of pose, and the natural and simple way in which he began talking to his guests, so as to get them on their own lines, which made him so charming a host to a stranger. His happy choice of matter for talk seemed to flow out of his sympathetic nature, and humble, vivid interest in other people's work.

To some, I think, he caused actual pain by his

---

[1] *Darwin considéré au point de vue des causes de son succès* (Geneva, 1882).

modesty ; I have seen the late Francis Balfour quite discomposed by having knowledge ascribed to himself on a point about which my father claimed to be utterly ignorant.

It is difficult to seize on the characteristics of my father's conversation.

He had more dread than have most people of repeating his stories, and continually said, " You must have heard me tell," or " I daresay I've told you." One peculiarity he had, which gave a curious effect to his conversation. The first few words of a sentence would often remind him of some exception to, or some reason against, what he was going to say ; and this again brought up some other point, so that the sentence would become a system of parenthesis within parenthesis, and it was often impossible to understand the drift of what he was saying until he came to the end of his sentence. He used to say of himself that he was not quick enough to hold an argument with any one, and I think this was true. Unless it was a subject on which he was just then at work, he could not get the train of argument into working order quickly enough. This is shown even in his letters ; thus, in the case of two letters to Professor Semper about the effect of isolation, he did not recall the series of facts he wanted until some days after the first letter had been sent off.

When puzzled in talking, he had a peculiar stammer on the first word of a sentence. I only recall this occurring with words beginning with w ; possibly he had a special difficulty with this letter, for I have heard him say that as a boy he could not pronounce w, and that sixpence was offered him if he could say "white wine," which he pronounced "rite rine." Possibly he may have inherited this tendency from Erasmus Darwin who stammered.[1]

He sometimes combined his metaphors in a curious way, using such a phrase as "holding on like life," —a mixture of "holding on for his life," and "holding on like grim death." It came from his eager way of putting emphasis into what he was saying. This sometimes gave an air of exaggeration where it was not intended; but it gave, too, a noble air of strong and generous conviction; as, for instance, when he gave his evidence before the Royal Commission on vivisection, and came out with his words about cruelty, "It deserves detestation and abhorrence." When he felt strongly about any similar question, he could hardly trust himself to speak, as he then easily became angry, a thing which he disliked excessively. He was conscious that his anger had a tendency to multiply itself in the utterance, and for this reason dreaded (for example) having to reprove a servant.

It was a proof of the modesty of his manner of talking, that when, for instance, a number of visitors came over from Sir John Lubbock's for a Sunday afternoon call, he never seemed to be preaching or lecturing, although he had so much of the talk to himself. He was particularly charming when "chaffing" any one, and in high spirits over it. His

[1] My father related a Johnsonian answer of Erasmus Darwin's : " Don't you find it very inconvenient stammering, Dr. Darwin ? " " No, Sir, because I have time to think before I speak, and don't ask impertinent questions."

manner at such times was light-hearted and boyish, and his refinement of nature came out most strongly. So, when he was talking to a lady who pleased and amused him, the combination of raillery and deference in his manner was delightful to see. There was a personal dignity about him, which the most familiar intercourse did not diminish. One felt that he was the last person with whom any one would wish to take a liberty, nor do I remember an instance of such a thing occurring to him.

When my father had several guests he managed them well, getting a talk with each, or bringing two or three together round his chair. In these conversations there was always a good deal of fun, and, speaking generally, there was either a humorous turn in his talk, or a sunny geniality which served instead. Perhaps my recollection of a pervading element of humour is the more vivid, because the best talks were with Mr. Huxley, in whom there is the aptness which is akin to humour, even when humour itself is not there. My father enjoyed Mr. Huxley's humour exceedingly, and would often say, " What splendid fun Huxley is ! " I think he probably had more scientific argument (of the nature of a fight) with Lyell and Sir Joseph Hooker.

He used to say that it grieved him to find that for the friends of his later life he had not the warm affection of his youth. Certainly in his early letters from Cambridge he gives proofs of strong friendship for Herbert and Fox ; but no one except himself would have said that his affection for his friends was not, throughout life, of the warmest possible kind. In serving a friend he would not spare him-

self, and precious time and strength were willingly
given. He undoubtedly had, to an unusual degree,
the power of attaching his friends to him. He had
many warm friendships, but to Sir Joseph Hooker
he was bound by ties of affection stronger than we
often see among men. He wrote in his *Recollections*,
" I have known hardly any man more lovable than
Hooker."

His relationship to the village people was a pleasant
one ; he treated them, one and all, with courtesy,
when he came in contact with them, and took an
interest in all relating to their welfare. Some time
after he came to live at Down he helped to found a
Friendly Club, and served as treasurer for thirty
years. He took much trouble about the club, keeping its accounts with minute and scrupulous exact-
ness, and taking pleasure in its prosperous condition.
Every Whit-Monday the club marched round with
band and banner and paraded on the lawn in front
of the house. There he met them, and explained
to them their financial position in a little speech
seasoned with a few well-worn jokes. He was often
unwell enough to make even this little ceremony
an exertion, but I think he never failed to meet
them.

He was also treasurer of the Coal Club, which gave
him a certain amount of work, and he acted for some
years as a County Magistrate.

With regard to my father's interest in the affairs
of the village, Mr. Brodie Innes has been so good as
to give me his recollections :—

" On my becoming Vicar of Down in 1846, we
became friends, and so continued till his death. His

conduct towards me and my family was one of unvarying kindness, and we repaid it by warm affection.

" In all parish matters he was an active assistant ;
in matters connected with the schools, charities, and
other business, his liberal contribution was ever
ready, and in the differences which at times occurred
in that, as in other parishes, I was always sure of
his support. He held that where there was really
no important objection, his assistance should be
given to the clergyman, who ought to know the
circumstances best, and was chiefly responsible."

His intercourse with strangers was marked with
scrupulous and rather formal politeness, but in fact
he had few opportunities of meeting strangers, and
the quiet life he led at Down made him feel confused
in a large gathering ; for instance, at the Royal
Society's *soirées* he felt oppressed by the numbers.
The feeling that he ought to know people, and the
difficulty he had in remembering faces in his latter
years, also added to his discomfort on such occasions.
He did not realise that he would be recognised from
his photographs, and I remember his being uneasy
at being obviously recognised by a stranger at the
Crystal Palace Aquarium.

I must say something of his manner of working :
a striking characteristic was his respect for time ;
he never forgot how precious it was. This was shown,
for instance, in the way in which he tried to curtail
his holidays ; also, and more clearly, with respect
to shorter periods. He would often say, that saving
the minutes was the way to get work done ; he
showed this love of saving the minutes in the difference he felt between a quarter of an hour and ten

minutes' work ; he never wasted a few spare minutes from thinking that it was not worth while to set to work. I was often struck by his way of working up to the very limit of his strength, so that he suddenly stopped in dictating, with the words, " I believe I mustn't do any more." The same eager desire not to lose time was seen in his quick movements when at work. I particularly remember noticing this when he was making an experiment on the roots of beans, which required some care in manipulation ; fastening the little bits of card upon the roots was done carefully and necessarily slowly, but the intermediate movements were all quick ; taking a fresh bean, seeing that the root was healthy, impaling it on a pin, fixing it on a cork, and seeing that it was vertical, &c. ; all these processes were performed with a kind of restrained eagerness. He gave one the impression of working with pleasure, and not with any drag. I have an image, too, of him as he recorded the result of some experiment, looking eagerly at each root, &c., and then writing with equal eagerness. I remember the quick movement of his head up and down as he looked from the object to the notes.

He saved a great deal of time through not having to do things twice. Although he would patiently go on repeating experiments where there was any good to be gained, he could not endure having to repeat an experiment which ought, if complete care had been taken, to have told its story at first—and this gave him a continual anxiety that the experiment should not be wasted ; he felt the experiment to be sacred, however slight a one it was. He wished to learn as much as possible from an experiment, so that he did not confine himself to observing the single point to which the experiment was directed, and his power of seeing a number of other things was wonderful. I do not think he cared for preliminary or rough observations intended to serve as guides and to be repeated. Any experiment done was to be of some use, and in this connection I remember how strongly he urged the necessity of keeping the notes of experiments which failed, and to this rule he always adhered.

In the literary part of his work he had the same horror of losing time, and the same zeal in what he was doing at the moment, and this made him careful not to be obliged unnecessarily to read anything a second time.

His natural tendency was to use simple methods and few instruments. The use of the compound microscope has much increased since his youth, and this at the expense of the simple one. It strikes us nowadays as extraordinary that he should have had no compound microscope when he went his *Beagle* voyage ; but in this he followed the advice of Robert Brown, who was an authority in such matters. He always had a great liking for the simple microscope, and maintained that nowadays it was too much neglected, and that one ought always to see as much as possible with the simple before taking to the compound microscope. In one of his letters he speaks on this point, and remarks that he suspects the work of a man who never uses the simple microscope.

His dissecting-table was a thick board, let into a

window of the study ; it was lower than an ordinary
table, so that he could not have worked at it standing ; but this, from wishing to save his strength, he
would not have done in any case. He sat at his
dissecting-table on a curious low stool which had
belonged to his father, with a seat revolving on a
vertical spindle, and mounted on large castors, so
that he could turn easily from side to side. His
ordinary tools, &c., were lying about on the table,
but besides these a number of odds and ends were
kept in a round table full of radiating drawers, and
turning on a vertical axis, which stood close by his
left side, as he sat at his microscope-table. The
drawers were labelled, " best tools," " rough tools,"
" specimens," " preparations for specimens," &c.
The most marked peculiarity of the contents of these
drawers was the care with which little scraps and
almost useless things were preserved ; he held the
well-known belief, that if you threw a thing away
you were sure to want it directly—and so things
accumulated.

If any one had looked at his tools, &c., lying on
the table, he would have been struck by an air of
simpleness, make-shift, and oddity.

At his right hand were shelves, with a number of
other odds and ends, glasses, saucers, tin biscuit boxes
for germinating seeds, zinc labels, saucers full of sand,
&c., &c. Considering how tidy and methodical he
was in essential things, it is curious that he bore
with so many make-shifts : for instance, instead of
having a box made of a desired shape, and stained
black inside, he would hunt up something like what
he wanted and get it darkened inside with shoe-

blacking; he did not care to have glass covers made for tumblers in which he germinated seeds, but used broken bits of irregular shape, with perhaps a narrow angle sticking uselessly out on one side. But so much of his experimenting was of a simple kind, that he had no need for any elaboration, and I think his habit in this respect was in great measure due to his desire to husband his strength, and not waste it on inessential things.

His way of marking objects may here be mentioned. If he had a number of things to distinguish, such as leaves, flowers, &c., he tied threads of different colours round them. In particular he used this method when he had only two classes of objects to distinguish; thus in the case of crossed and self-fertilised flowers, one set would be marked with black and one with white thread, tied round the stalk of the flower. I remember well the look of two sets of capsules, gathered and waiting to be weighed, counted, &c., with pieces of black and of white thread to distinguish the trays in which they lay. When he had to compare two sets of seedlings, sowed in the same pot, he separated them by a partition of zinc-plate; and the zinc-label, which gave the necessary details about the experiment, was always placed on a certain side, so that it became instinctive with him to know without reading the label which were the "crossed" and which the "self-fertilised."

His love of each particular experiment, and his eager zeal not to lose the fruit of it, came out markedly in these crossing experiments—in the elaborate care he took not to make any confusion in putting capsules into wrong trays, &c., &c. I can recall his appearance as he counted seeds under the simple microscope with an alertness not usually characterising such mechanical work as counting. I think he personified each seed as a small demon trying to elude him by getting into the wrong heap, or jumping away altogether; and this gave to the work the excitement of a game. He had great faith in instruments, and I do not think it naturally occurred to him to doubt the accuracy of a scale, a measuring glass, &c. He was astonished when we found that one of his micrometers differed from the other. He did not require any great accuracy in most of his measurements, and had not good scales; he had an old three-foot rule, which was the common property of the household, and was constantly being borrowed, because it was the only one which was certain to be in its place—unless, indeed, the last borrower had forgotten to put it back. For measuring the height of plants, he had a seven-foot deal rod, graduated by the village carpenter. Latterly he took to using paper scales graduated to millimeters. I do not mean by this account of his instruments that any of his experiments suffered from want of accuracy in measurement, I give them as examples of his simple methods and faith in others—faith at least in instrument-makers, whose whole trade was a mystery to him.

A few of his mental characteristics, bearing especially on his mode of working, occur to me. There was one quality of mind which seemed to be of special and extreme advantage in leading him to make discoveries. It was the power of never letting exceptions pass unnoticed. Everybody notices a fact as an exception when it is striking or frequent, but he had a special instinct for arresting an exception. A point apparently slight and unconnected with his present work is passed over by many a man almost unconsciously with some half-considered explanation, which is in fact no explanation. It was just these things that he seized on to make a start from. In a certain sense there is nothing special in this procedure, many discoveries being made by means of it. I only mention it because, as I watched him at work, the value of this power to an experimenter was so strongly impressed upon me.

Another quality which was shown in his experimental work, was his power of sticking to a subject ; he used almost to apologise for his patience, saying that he could not bear to be beaten, as if this were rather a sign of weakness on his part. He often quoted the saying, " It's dogged as does it ; " and I think doggedness expresses his frame of mind almost better than perseverance. Perseverance seems hardly to express his almost fierce desire to force the truth to reveal itself. He often said that it was important that a man should know the right point at which to give up an inquiry. And I think it was his tendency to pass this point that inclined him to apologise for his perseverance, and gave the air of doggedness to his work.

He often said that no one could be a good observer unless he was an active theoriser. This brings me back to what I said about his instinct for arresting exceptions : it was as though he were charged with theorising power ready to flow into any channel on the slightest disturbance, so that no fact, however small, could avoid releasing a stream of theory, and thus the fact became magnified into importance. In this way it naturally happened that many untenable theories occurred to him; but fortunately his richness of imagination was equalled by his power of judging and condemning the thoughts that occurred to him. He was just to his theories, and did not condemn them unheard; and so it happened that he was willing to test what would seem to most people not at all worth testing. These rather wild trials he called "fool's experiments," and enjoyed extremely. As an example I may mention that finding the seed-leaves of a kind of sensitive plant, to be highly sensitive to vibrations of the table, he fancied that they might perceive the vibrations of sound, and therefore made me play my bassoon close to a plant.[1]

The love of experiment was very strong in him, and I can remember the way he would say, " I shan't be easy till I have tried it," as if an outside force were driving him. He enjoyed experimenting much more than work which only entailed reasoning, and when he was engaged on one of his books which required argument and the marshalling of facts, he felt experimental work to be a rest or holiday. Thus, while working upon the *Variations of Animals and Plants* in 1860–61, he made out the fertilisation of Orchids, and thought himself idle for giving so much time to them. It is interesting to think that so important a piece of research should have been under-

[1] This is not so much an example of superabundant theorising from a small cause as of his wish to test the most improbable ideas.

taken and largely worked out as a pastime in place of more serious work. The letters to Hooker of this period contain expressions such as, " God forgive me for being so idle ; I am quite sillily interested in the work." The intense pleasure he took in understanding the adaptations for fertilisation is strongly shown in these letters. He speaks in one of his letters of his intention of working at Sundew as a rest from the *Descent of Man*. He has described in his *Recollections* the strong satisfaction he felt in solving the problem of heterostylism.[1] And I have heard him mention that the Geology of South America gave him almost more pleasure than anything else. It was perhaps this delight in work requiring keen observation that made him value praise given to his observing powers almost more than appreciation of his other qualities.

For books he had no respect, but merely considered them as tools to be worked with. Thus he did not bind them, and even when a paper book fell to pieces from use, as happened to Müller's *Befruchtung*, he preserved it from complete dissolution by putting a metal clip over its back. In the same way he would cut a heavy book in half, to make it more convenient to hold. He used to boast that he had made Lyell publish the second edition of one of his books in two volumes, instead of one, by telling him how he had been obliged to cut it in half. Pamphlets were often treated even more severely than books, for he would tear out, for the sake of saving room, all the pages except the one that interested him. The consequence

---

[1] That is to say, the sexual relations in such plants as the cowslip.

of all this was, that his library was not ornamental, but was striking from being so evidently a working collection of books.

He was methodical in his manner of reading books and pamphlets bearing on his own work. He had one shelf on which were piled up the books he had not yet read, and another to which they were transferred after having been read, and before being catalogued. He would often groan over his unread books, because there were so many which he knew he should never read. Many a book was at once transferred to the other heap, either marked with a cypher at the end, to show that it contained no marked passages, or inscribed, perhaps, " not read," or " only skimmed." The books accumulated in the " read " heap until the shelves overflowed, and then, with much lamenting, a day was given up to the cataloguing. He disliked this work, and as the necessity of undertaking the work became imperative, would often say, in a voice of despair, " We really must do these books soon."

In each book, as he read it, he marked passages bearing on his work. In reading a book or pamphlet, &c., he made pencil-lines at the side of the page, often adding short remarks, and at the end made a list of the pages marked. When it was to be catalogued and put away, the marked pages were looked at, and so a rough abstract of the book was made. This abstract would perhaps be written under three or four headings on different sheets, the facts being sorted out and added to the previously collected facts in the different subjects. He had other sets of abstracts arranged, not according to subject, but according to the periodicals from which they were taken. When collecting facts on a large scale, in earlier years, he used to read through, and make abstracts, in this way, of whole series of journals.

In some of his early letters he speaks of filling several note-books with facts for his book on species ; but it was certainly early that he adopted his plan of using portfolios, as described in the *Recollections*. My father and M. de Candolle were mutually pleased to discover that they had adopted the same plan of classifying facts. De Candolle describes the method in his *Phytologie*, and in his sketch of my father mentions the satisfaction he felt in seeing it in action at Down.

Besides these portfolios, of which there are some dozens full of notes, there are large bundles of MS. marked " used " and put away. He felt the value of his notes, and had a horror of their destruction by fire. I remember, when some alarm of fire had happened, his begging me to be especially careful, adding very earnestly, that the rest of his life would be miserable if his notes and books were destroyed.

He shows the same feeling in writing about the loss of a manuscript, the purport of his words being, " I have a copy, or the loss would have killed me." In writing a book he would spend much time and labour in making a skeleton or plan of the whole, and in enlarging and sub-classing each heading as described in his *Recollections*. I think this careful arrangement of the plan was not at all essential to the building up of his argument, but for its present-ment, and for the arrangement of his facts. In his *Life of Erasmus Darwin*, as it was first printed in slips, the growth of the book from a skeleton was plainly visible. The arrangement was altered afterwards, because it was too formal and categorical, and seemed to give the character of his grandfather rather by means of a list of qualities than as a complete picture.

It was only within the last few years that he adopted a plan of writing which he was convinced suited him best, and which is described in the *Recollections* ; namely, writing a rough copy straight off without the slightest attention to style. It was characteristic of him that he felt unable to write with sufficient want of care if he used his best paper, and thus it was that he wrote on the backs of old proofs or manuscript. The rough copy was then reconsidered, and a fair copy was made. For this purpose he had foolscap paper ruled at wide intervals, the lines being needed to prevent him writing so closely that correction became difficult. The fair copy was then corrected, and was recopied before being sent to the printers. The copying was done by Mr. E. Norman, who began this work many years ago when village schoolmaster at Down. My father became so used to Mr. Norman's handwriting, that he could not correct manuscript, even when clearly written out by one of his children, until it had been recopied by Mr. Norman. The MS., on returning from Mr. Norman, was once more corrected, and then sent off to the printers. Then came the work of revising and correcting the proofs, which my father found especially wearisome.

When the book was passing through the " slip " stage he was glad to have corrections and suggestions from others. Thus my mother looked over the proofs of the *Origin*. In some of the later works my sister, Mrs. Litchfield, did much of the correction. After my sister's marriage perhaps most of the work fell to my share.

My sister, Mrs. Litchfield, writes :—

" This work was very interesting in itself, and it was inexpressibly exhilarating to work for him. He was so ready to be convinced that any suggested alteration was an improvement, and so full of gratitude for the trouble taken. I do not think that he ever forgot to tell me what improvement he thought I had made, and he used almost to excuse himself if he did not agree with any correction. I think I felt the singular modesty and graciousness of his nature through thus working for him in a way I never should otherwise have done."

Perhaps the commonest corrections needed were of obscurities due to the omission of a necessary link in the reasoning, evidently omitted through familiarity with the subject. Not that there was any fault in the sequence of the thoughts, but that from familiarity with his argument he did not notice when the words failed to reproduce his thought. He also frequently put too much matter into one sentence, so that it had to be cut up into two.

On the whole, I think the pains which my father took over the literary part of the work were very remarkable. He often laughed or grumbled at himself for the difficulty which he found in writing English, saying, for instance, that if a bad arrangement of a sentence was possible, he should be sure to adopt it. He once got much amusement and satisfaction out of the difficulty which one of the family found in writing a short circular. He had the pleasure of correcting and laughing at obscurities, involved sentences, and other defects, and thus took his revenge for all the criticism he had himself to bear with. He would quote with astonishment Miss Martineau's advice to young authors, to write straight off and send the MS. to the printer without correction. But in some cases he acted in a somewhat similar manner. When a sentence became hopelessly involved, he would ask himself, " now what *do* you want to say ? " and his answer written down, would often disentangle the confusion.

His style has been much praised ; on the other hand, at least one good judge has remarked to me that it is not a good style. It is, above all things, direct and clear ; and it is characteristic of himself in its simplicity bordering on naïveté, and in its absence of pretence. He had the strongest disbelief in the common idea that a classical scholar must write good English ; indeed, he thought that the contrary was the case. In writing, he sometimes showed the same tendency to strong expressions that he did in conversation. Thus in the *Origin,* p. 440, there is a description of a larval cirripede, " with six pairs of beautifully constructed natatory legs, a pair of magnificent compound eyes, and extremely complex antennæ." We used to laugh at him for this sentence, which we compared to an advertisement. This tendency to give himself up to the enthusiastic turn of his thought without fear of being ludicrous appears elsewhere in his writings.

His courteous and conciliatory tone towards his

reader is remarkable, and it must be partly this quality which revealed his personal sweetness of character to so many who had never seen him. I have always felt it to be a curious fact, that he who has altered the face of Biological Science, and is in this respect the chief of the moderns, should have written and worked in so essentially a non-modern spirit and manner. In reading his books one is reminded of the older naturalists rather than of any modern school of writers. He was a Naturalist in the old sense of the word, that is, a man who works at many branches of science, not merely a specialist in one. Thus it is, that, though he founded whole new divisions of special subjects—such as the fertilisation of flowers, insectivorous plants, &c.—yet even in treating these very subjects he does not strike the reader as a specialist. The reader feels like a friend who is being talked to by a courteous gentleman, not like a pupil being lectured by a professor. The tone of such a book as the *Origin* is charming, and almost pathetic ; it is the tone of a man who, convinced of the truth of his own views, hardly expects to convince others ; it is just the reverse of the style of a fanatic, who tries to force belief on his readers. The reader is never scorned for any amount of doubt which he may be imagined to feel, and his scepticism is treated with patient respect. A sceptical reader, or perhaps even an unreasonable reader, seems to have been generally present to his thoughts. It was in consequence of this feeling, perhaps, that he took much trouble over points which he imagined would strike the reader, or save him trouble, and so tempt him to read.

For the same reason he took much interest in the illustrations of his books, and I think rated rather too highly their value. The illustrations for his earlier books were drawn by professional artists. This was the case in *Animals and Plants*, the *Descent of Man*, and the *Expression of the Emotions*. On the other hand, *Climbing Plants*, *Insectivorous Plants*, the *Movements of Plants*, and *Forms of Flowers*, were, to a large extent, illustrated by some of his children—my brother George having drawn by far the most. It was delightful to draw for him, as he was enthusiastic in his praise of very moderate performances. I remember well his charming manner of receiving the drawings of one of his daughters-in-law, and how he would finish his words of praise by saying, " Tell A——, Michael Angelo is nothing to it." Though he praised so generously, he always looked closely at the drawing, and easily detected mistakes or carelessness.

He had a horror of being lengthy, and seems to have been really much annoyed and distressed when he found how the *Variations of Animals and Plants* was growing under his hands. I remember his cordially agreeing with ' Tristram Shandy's ' words, " Let no man say, ' Come, I'll write a duodecimo.' "

His consideration for other authors was as marked a characteristic as his tone towards his reader. He speaks of all other authors as persons deserving of respect. In cases where, as in the case of ——'s experiments on Drosera, he thought lightly of the author, he speaks of him in such a way that no one would suspect it. In other cases he treats the confused writings of ignorant persons as though the fault lay with himself for not appreciating or understanding them. Besides this general tone of respect, he had a pleasant way of expressing his opinion on the value of a quoted work, or his obligation for a piece of private information.

His respectful feeling was not only admirable, but was I think of practical use in making him ready to consider the ideas and observations of all manner of people. He used almost to apologise for this, and would say that he was at first inclined to rate everything too highly.

It was a great merit in his mind that, in spite of having so strong a respectful feeling towards what he read, he had the keenest of instincts as to whether a man was trustworthy or not. He seemed to form a very definite opinion as to the accuracy of the men whose books he read ; and employed this judgment in his choice of facts for use in argument or as illustrations. I gained the impression that he felt this power of judging of a man's trustworthiness to be of much value.

He had a keen feeling of the sense of honour that ought to reign among authors, and had a horror of any kind of laxness in quoting. He had a contempt for the love of honour and glory, and in his letters often blames himself for the pleasure he took in the success of his books, as though he were departing from his ideal—a love of truth and carelessness about fame. Often, when writing to Sir J. Hooker what he calls a boasting letter, he laughs at himself for his conceit and want of modesty. A wonderfully interesting letter is given in Chapter X. of the *Life*, bequeathing to my mother, in case of his death, the care of publishing the manuscript of his first essay on evolution. This letter seems to me full of an intense desire that his theory should succeed as a contribution to knowledge, and apart from any desire for personal fame. He certainly had the healthy desire for success which a man of strong feelings ought to have. But at the time of the publication of the *Origin* it is evident that he was overwhelmingly satisfied with the adherence of such men as Lyell, Hooker, Huxley, and Asa Gray, and did not dream of or desire any such general fame as that to which he attained.

Connected with his contempt for the undue love of fame, was an equally strong dislike of all questions of priority. The letters to Lyell, at the time of the *Origin*, show the anger he felt with himself for not being able to repress a feeling of disappointment at what he thought was Mr. Wallace's forestalling of all his years of work. His sense of literary honour comes out strongly in these letters ; and his feeling about priority is again shown in the admiration expressed in his *Recollections* of Mr. Wallace's self-annihilation.

His feeling about reclamations, including answers to attacks and all kinds of discussions, was strong. It is simply expressed in a letter to Falconer (1863) : " If I ever felt angry towards you, for whom I have a sincere friendship, I should begin to suspect that I was a little mad. I was very sorry about your reclamation, as I think it is in every case a mistake and should be left to others. Whether I should so act myself under provocation is a different question." It was a feeling partly dictated by instinctive delicacy, and partly by a strong sense of the waste of time, energy, and temper thus caused. He said that he owed his determination not to get into discussions [1] to the advice of Lyell,—advice which he transmitted to those among his friends who were given to paper warfare.

If the character of my father's working life is to be understood, the conditions of ill-health, under which he worked, must be constantly borne in mind. He bore his illness with such uncomplaining patience, that even his children can hardly, I believe, realise the extent of his habitual suffering. In their case the difficulty is heightened by the fact that, from the days of their earliest recollections, they saw him in constant ill-health,—and saw him, in spite of it, full of pleasure in what pleased them. Thus, in later life, their perception of what he endured had to be disentangled from the impression produced in childhood by constant genial kindness under conditions of unrecognised difficulty. No one indeed, except my mother, knows the full amount of suffering he endured, or the full amount of his wonderful patience. For all the latter years of his life she never left him for a night ; and her days were so planned that all his resting hours might be shared with her. She shielded him from every avoidable annoyance, and

---

[1] He departed from his rule in his " Note on the Habits of the Pampas Woodpecker, *Colaptes campestris*," *Proc. Zool. Soc.*, 1870, p. 705 : also in a letter published in the *Athenæum* (1863, p. 554), in which case he afterwards regretted that he had not remained silent. His replies to criticisms, in the later editions of the *Origin*, can hardly be classed as infractions of his rule.

omitted nothing that might save him trouble, or prevent him becoming overtired, or that might alleviate the many discomforts of his ill-health. I hesitate to speak thus freely of a thing so sacred as the life-long devotion which prompted all this constant and tender care. But it is, I repeat, a principal feature of his life, that for nearly forty years he never knew one day of the health of ordinary men, and that thus his life was one long struggle against the weariness and strain of sickness. And this cannot be told without speaking of the one condition which enabled him to bear the strain and fight out the struggle to the end.

II

THE RELIGION OF CHARLES DARWIN

My father in his published works was reticent on the matter of religion, and what he has left on the subject was not written with a view to publication.[1]

I believe that his reticence arose from several causes He felt strongly that a man's religion is an essentially private matter, and one concerning himself alone. This is indicated by the following extract from a letter of 1879[2] :—

"What my own views may be is a question of no consequence to any one but myself. But, as you ask, I may state that my judgment often fluctuates. . . . In my most extreme fluctuations I have never been an Atheist in the sense of denying the existence of a God. I think that generally (and more and more as I grow older), but not always, that an Agnostic would be the more correct description of my state of mind."

He naturally shrank from wounding the sensibilities of others in religious matters, and he was also

[1] As an exception, may be mentioned a few words of concurrence with Dr. Abbott's *Truths for the Times*, which my father allowed to be published in the *Index*.

[2] Addressed to Mr. J. Fordyce, and published by him in his *Aspects of Scepticism*, 1883.

influenced by the consciousness that a man ought not to publish on a subject to which he has not given special and continuous thought. That he felt this caution to apply to himself in the matter of religion is shown in a letter to Dr. F. E. Abbott, of Cambridge, U.S. (September 6, 1871). After explaining that the weakness arising from bad health prevented him from feeling "equal to deep reflection, on the deepest subject which can fill a man's mind," he goes on to say: "With respect to my former notes to you, I quite forget their contents. I have to write many letters, and can reflect but little on what I write; but I fully believe and hope that I have never written a word, which at the time I did not think; but I think you will agree with me, that anything which is to be given to the public ought to be maturely weighed and cautiously put. It never occurred to me that you would wish to print any extract from my notes: if it had, I would have kept a copy. I put 'private' from habit, only as yet partially acquired, from some hasty notes of mine having been printed, which were not in the least degree worth printing, though otherwise unobjectionable. It is simply ridiculous to suppose that my former note to you would be worth sending to me, with any part marked which you desire to print; but if you like to do so, I will at once say whether I should have any objection. I feel in some degree unwilling to express myself publicly on religious subjects, as I do not feel that I have thought deeply enough to justify any publicity."

What follows is from another letter to Dr. Abbott (November 16, 1871), in which my father gives more fully his reasons for not feeling competent to write on religious and moral subjects :—

"I can say with entire truth that I feel honoured by your request that I should become a contributor to the *Index*, and am much obliged for the draft. I fully, also, subscribe to the proposition that it is the duty of every one to spread what he believes to be the truth ; and I honour you for doing so, with so much devotion and zeal. But I cannot comply with your request for the following reasons ; and excuse me for giving them in some detail, as I should be very sorry to appear in your eyes ungracious. My health is very weak : I *never* pass 24 hours without many hours of discomfort, when I can do nothing whatever. I have thus, also, lost two whole consecutive months this season. Owing to this weakness, and my head being often giddy, I am unable to master new subjects requiring much thought, and can deal only with old materials. At no time am I a quick thinker or writer ; whatever I have done in science has solely been by long pondering, patience and industry.

"Now I have never systematically thought much on religion in relation to science, or on morals in relation to society ; and without steadily keeping my mind on such subjects for a long period, I am really incapable of writing anything worth sending to the *Index*."

He was more than once asked to give his views on religion, and he had, as a rule, no objection to doing so in a private letter. Thus, in answer to a Dutch student, he wrote (April 2, 1873) :—

"I am sure you will excuse my writing at length,

when I tell you that I have long been much out of health, and am now staying away from my home for rest.

"It is impossible to answer your question briefly; and I am not sure that I could do so, even if I wrote at some length. But I may say that the impossibility of conceiving that this grand and wondrous universe, with our conscious selves, arose through chance, seems to me the chief argument for the existence of God; but whether this is an argument of real value, I have never been able to decide. I am aware that if we admit a First Cause, the mind still craves to know whence it came, and how it arose. Nor can I overlook the difficulty from the immense amount of suffering through the world. I am, also, induced to defer to a certain extent to the judgment of the many able men who have fully believed in God; but here again I see how poor an argument this is. The safest conclusion seems to me that the whole subject is beyond the scope of man's intellect; but man can do his duty."

Again in 1879 he was applied to by a German student, in a similar manner. The letter was answered by a member of my father's family, who wrote:—

"Mr. Darwin begs me to say that he receives so many letters, that he cannot answer them all.

"He considers that the theory of Evolution is quite compatible with the belief in a God; but that you must remember that different persons have different definitions of what they mean by God."

This, however, did not satisfy the German youth, who again wrote to my father, and received from him the following reply:—

" I am much engaged, an old man, and out of health, and I cannot spare time to answer your questions fully,—nor indeed can they be answered. Science has nothing to do with Christ, except in so far as the habit of scientific research makes a man cautious in admitting evidence. For myself, I do not believe that there ever has been any revelation. As for a future life, every man must judge for himself between conflicting vague probabilities."

The passages which here follow are extracts, somewhat abbreviated, from a part of the Autobiography, written in 1876, in which my father gives the history of his religious views :—

" During these two years [1] I was led to think much about religion. Whilst on board the *Beagle* I was quite orthodox, and I remember being heartily laughed at by several of the officers (though themselves orthodox) for quoting the Bible as an unanswerable authority on some point of morality. I suppose it was the novelty of the argument that amused them. But I had gradually come by this time, *i.e.* 1836 to 1839, to see that the Old Testament was no more to be trusted than the sacred books of the Hindoos. The question then continually rose before my mind and would not be banished,—is it credible that if God were now to make a revelation to the Hindoos, he would permit it to be connected with the belief in Vishnu, Siva, &c., as Christianity is connected with the Old Testament ? This appeared to me utterly incredible.

" By further reflecting that the clearest evidence would be requisite to make any sane man believe in

[1] October 1836 to January 1839.

the miracles by which Christianity is supported,—and that the more we know of the fixed laws of nature the more incredible do miracles become,—that the men at that time were ignorant and credulous to a degree almost incomprehensible by us,—that the Gospels cannot be proved to have been written simultaneously with the events,—that they differ in many important details, far too important, as it seemed to me, to be admitted as the usual inaccuracies of eye-witnesses ;—by such reflections as these, which I give not as having the least novelty or value, but as they influenced me, I gradually came to disbelieve in Christianity as a divine revelation. The fact that many false religions have spread over large portions of the earth like wildfire had some weight with me.

" But I was very unwilling to give up my belief ; I feel sure of this, for I can well remember often and often inventing day-dreams of old letters between distinguished Romans, and manuscripts being discovered at Pompeii or elsewhere, which confirmed in the most striking manner all that was written in the Gospels. But I found it more and more difficult, with free scope given to my imagination, to invent evidence which would suffice to convince me. Thus disbelief crept over me at a very slow rate, but was at last complete. The rate was so slow that I felt no distress.

" Although I did not think much about the existence of a personal God until a considerably later period of my life, I will here give the vague conclusions to which I have been driven. The old argument from design in Nature, as given by Paley, which formerly seemed to me so conclusive, fails, now that the law of natural selection has been discovered. We can no longer argue that, for instance, the beautiful hinge of a bivalve shell must have been made by an intelligent being, like the hinge of a door by man. There seems to be no more design in the variability of organic beings, and in the action of natural selection, than in the course which the wind blows. But I have discussed this subject at the end of my book on the *Variation of Domesticated Animals and Plants*,[1] and the argument there given has never, as far as I can see, been answered.

" But passing over the endless beautiful adaptations which we everywhere meet with, it may be asked how can the generally beneficent arrangement of the world be accounted for ? Some writers indeed are so much impressed with the amount of suffering in the world, that they doubt, if we look to all sentient beings, whether there is more of misery or of happiness ; whether the world as a whole is a good or a bad one. According to my judgment happiness decidedly prevails, though this would be very difficult to prove. If the truth of this conclusion be granted,

[1] My father asks whether we are to believe that the forms are preordained of the broken fragments of rock which are fitted together by man to build his houses. If not, why should we believe that the variations of domestic animals or plants are preordained for the sake of the breeder ? " But if we give up the principle in one case, . . . no shadow of reason can be assigned for the belief that variations alike in nature and the result of the same general laws, which have been the groundwork through natural selection of the formation of the most perfectly adapted animals in the world, man included, were intentionally and specially guided."—*Variation of Animals and Plants*, 1st Edit. vol. ii. p. 431.—F. D.

it harmonises well with the effects which we might expect from natural selection. If all the individuals of any species were habitually to suffer to an extreme degree, they would neglect to propagate their kind; but we have no reason to believe that this has ever, or at least often occurred. Some other considerations, moreover, lead to the belief that all sentient beings have been formed so as to enjoy, as a general rule, happiness.

" Every one who believes, as I do, that all the corporeal and mental organs (excepting those which are neither advantageous nor disadvantageous to the possessor) of all beings have been developed through natural selection, or the survival of the fittest, together with use or habit, will admit that these organs have been formed so that their possessors may compete successfully with other beings, and thus increase in number. Now an animal may be led to pursue that course of action which is most beneficial to the species by suffering, such as pain, hunger, thirst, and fear; or by pleasure, as in eating and drinking, and in the propagation of the species, &c.; or by both means combined, as in the search for food. But pain or suffering of any kind, if long continued, causes depression and lessens the power of action, yet is well adapted to make a creature guard itself against any great or sudden evil. Pleasurable sensations, on the other hand, may be long continued without any depressing effect; on the contrary, they stimulate the whole system to increased action. Hence it has come to pass that most or all sentient beings have been developed in such a manner, through natural selection, that pleasurable sensations serve as their habitual guides. We see this in the pleasure from exertion, even occasionally from great exertion of the body or mind,—in the pleasure of our daily meals, and especially in the pleasure derived from sociability, and from loving our families. The sum of such pleasures as these, which are habitual or frequently recurrent, give, as I can hardly doubt, to most sentient beings an excess of happiness over misery, although many occasionally suffer much. Such suffering is quite compatible with the belief in Natural Selection, which is not perfect in its action, but tends only to render each species as successful as possible in the battle for life with other species, in wonderfully complex and changing circumstances.

" That there is much suffering in the world no one disputes. Some have attempted to explain this with reference to man by imagining that it serves for his moral improvement. But the number of men in the world is as nothing compared with that of all other sentient beings, and they often suffer greatly without any moral improvement. This very old argument from the existence of suffering against the existence of an intelligent First Cause seems to me a strong one ; whereas, as just remarked, the presence of much suffering agrees well with the view that all organic beings have been developed through variation and natural selection. ·

" At the present day the most usual argument for the existence of an intelligent God is drawn from the deep inward conviction and feelings which are experienced by most persons.

" Formerly I was led by feelings such as those just referred to (although I do not think that the religious.

sentiment was ever strongly developed in me), to the firm conviction of the existence of God and of the immortality of the soul. In my Journal I wrote that whilst standing in the midst of the grandeur of a Brazilian forest, ' it is not possible to give an adequate idea of the higher feelings of wonder, admiration, and devotion which fill and elevate the mind.' I well remember my conviction that there is more in man than the mere breath of his body ; but now the grandest scenes would not cause any such convictions and feelings to rise in my mind. It may be truly said that I am like a man who has become colour-blind, and the universal belief by men of the existence of redness makes my present loss of perception of not the least value as evidence. This argument would be a valid one if all men of all races had the same inward conviction of the existence of one God ; but we know that this is very far from being the case. Therefore I cannot see that such inward convictions and feelings are of any weight as evidence of what really exists. The state of mind which grand scenes formerly excited in me, and which was intimately connected with a belief in God, did not essentially differ from that which is often called the sense of sublimity ; and however difficult it may be to explain the genesis of this sense, it can hardly be advanced as an argument for the existence of God, any more than the powerful though vague and similar feelings excited by music.

" With respect to immortality, nothing shows me [so clearly] how strong and almost instinctive a belief it is as the consideration of the view now held by most physicists, namely, that the sun with all the planets will in time grow too cold for life, unless indeed some great body dashes into the sun and thus gives it fresh life. Believing as I do that man in the distant future will be a far more perfect creature than he now is, it is an intolerable thought that he and all other sentient beings are doomed to complete annihilation after such long-continued slow progress. To those who fully admit the immortality of the human soul, the destruction of our world will not appear so dreadful.

" Another source of conviction in the existence of God, connected with the reason and not with the feelings, impresses me as having much more weight. This follows from the extreme difficulty or rather impossibility of conceiving this immense and wonderful universe, including man with his capacity of looking far backwards and far into futurity, as the result of blind chance or necessity. When thus reflecting, I feel compelled to look to a First Cause having an intelligent mind in some degree analogous to that of man ; and I deserve to be called a Theist. This conclusion was strong in my mind about the time, as far as I can remember, when I wrote the *Origin of Species*, and it is since that time that it has very gradually, with many fluctuations, become weaker. But then arises the doubt—can the mind of man, which has, as I fully believe, been developed from a mind as low as that possessed by the lowest animals, be trusted when it draws such grand conclusions ?

" I cannot pretend to throw the least light on such abstruse problems. The mystery of the beginning of all things is insoluble by us, and I for one must be content to remain an Agnostic.''

APPENDIX II

The following letters repeat to some extent what is given above from the *Autobiography*. The first one refers to *The Boundaries of Science: a Dialogue*, published in *Macmillan's Magazine*, for July 1861.

C. D. to Miss Julia Wedgwood, July 11 [1861].

Some one has sent us *Macmillan*, and I must tell you how much I admire your Article, though at the same time I must confess that I could not clearly follow you in some parts, which probably is in main part due to my not being at all accustomed to metaphysical trains of thought. I think that you understand my book [1] perfectly, and that I find a very rare event with my critics. The ideas in the last page have several times vaguely crossed my mind. Owing to several correspondents, I have been led lately to think, or rather to try to think, over some of the chief points discussed by you. But the result has been with me a maze—something like thinking on the origin of evil, to which you allude. The mind refuses to look at this universe, being what it is, without having been designed; yet, where one would most expect design, viz. in the structure of a sentient being, the more I think on the subject, the less I can see proof of design. Asa Gray and some others look at each variation, or at least at each beneficial variation (which A. Gray would compare with the raindrops [2] which do not fall on the sea, but on to the land to fertilise it), as having been providentially

---

[1] The *Origin of Species*.

[2] Dr. Gray's rain-drop metaphor occurs in the Essay, *Darwin and his Reviewers* (*Darwiniana*, p. 157): " The whole animate life of a country depends absolutely upon the vegetation, the vegetation upon the rain. The moisture is furnished

designed. Yet when I ask him whether he looks at each variation in the rock-pigeon, by which man has made by accumulation a pouter or fantail pigeon, as providentially designed for man's' amusement, he does not know what to answer ; and if he, or any one, admits [that] these variations are accidental, as far as purpose is concerned (of course not accidental as to their cause or origin), then I can see no reason why he should rank the accumulated variations by which the beautifully-adapted woodpecker has been formed as providentially designed. For it would be easy to imagine the enlarged crop of the pouter, or tail of the fantail, as of some use to birds, in a state of nature, having peculiar habits of life. These are the considerations which perplex me about design ; but whether you will care to hear them, I know not.

On the subject of design, he wrote (July 1860) to Dr. Gray :

" One word more on 'designed laws' and ' unde-signed results.' I see a bird which I want for food, take my gun and kill it, I do this *designedly*. An innocent and good man stands under a tree and is killed by a flash of lightning. Do you believe (and I really should like to hear) that God *designedly* killed this man ? Many or most persons do believe this ; I can't and don't. If you believe so, do you

by the ocean, is raised by the sun's heat from the ocean's surface, and is wafted inland by the winds. But what multitudes of rain-drops fall back into the ocean—are as much without a final cause as the incipient varieties which come to nothing ! Does it therefore follow that the rains which are bestowed upon the soil with such rule and average regularity were not designed to support vegetable and animal life ? "

believe that when a swallow snaps up a gnat that God designed that that particular swallow should snap up that particular gnat at that particular instant ? I believe that the man and the gnat are in the same predicament. If the death of neither man nor gnat are designed, I see no good reason to believe that their *first* birth or production should be necessarily designed."

C. D. to W. Graham. Down, July 3rd, 1881.

DEAR SIR,—I hope that you will not think it intrusive on my part to thank you heartily for the pleasure which I have derived from reading your admirably-written *Creed of Science*, though I have not yet quite finished it, as now that I am old I read very slowly. It is a very long time since any other book has interested me so much. The work must have cost you several years and much hard labour with full leisure for work. You would not probably expect any one fully to agree with you on so many abstruse subjects ; and there are some points in your book which I cannot digest. The chief one is that the existence of so-called natural laws implies purpose. I cannot see this. Not to mention that many expect that the several great laws will some day be found to follow inevitably from some one single law, yet taking the laws as we now know them, and look at the moon, where the law of gravitation—and no doubt of the conservation of energy—of the atomic theory, &c., &c., hold good, and I cannot see that there is then necessarily any purpose. Would there be purpose if the lowest organisms alone, destitute of consciousness, existed in the moon ? But I have had no practice in abstract reasoning, and I may be all astray. Nevertheless you have expressed my inward conviction, though far more vividly and clearly than I could have done, that the Universe is not the result of chance.[1] But then with me the horrid doubt always arises whether the convictions of man's mind, which has been developed from the mind of the lower animals, are of any value or at all trustworthy. Would any one trust in the convictions of a monkey's mind, if there are any convictions in such a mind ? Secondly, I think that I could make somewhat of a case against the enormous importance which you attribute to our greatest men ; I have been accustomed to think second, third, and fourth-rate men of very high importance, at least in the case of Science. Lastly, I could show fight on natural selection having done and doing more for the progress of civilisation than you seem inclined to admit. Remember what risk the nations of Europe ran, not so many centuries ago, of being overwhelmed by the Turks, and how ridiculous such an idea now is ! The more civilised so-called Caucasian races have beaten the Turkish

[1] The Duke of Àrgyll (*Good Words*, April 1885, p. 244) has recorded a few words on this subject, spoken by my father in the last year of his life. " . . . in the course of that conversation I said to Mr. Darwin, with reference to some of his own remarkable works on the *Fertilisation of Orchids*, and upon *The Earthworms*, and various other observations he made of the wonderful contrivances for certain purposes in nature—I said it was impossible to look at these without seeing that they were the effect and the expression of mind. I shall never forget Mr. Darwin's answer. He looked at me very hard and said, ' Well, that often comes over me with overwhelming force ; but at other times,' and he shook his head vaguely, adding, ' it seems to go away.' "

hollow in the struggle for existence. Looking to the world at no very distant date, what an endless number of the lower races will have been eliminated by the higher civilised races throughout the world. But I will write no more, and not even mention the many points in your work which have much interested me. I have indeed cause to apologise for troubling you with my impressions, and my sole excuse is the excitement in my mind which your book has aroused.

I beg leave to remain, dear sir,

Yours faithfully and obliged.

Darwin spoke little on these subjects, and I can contribute nothing from my own recollection of his conversation which can add to the impression here given of his attitude towards Religion.[1] Some further idea of his views may, however, be gathered from occasional remarks in his letters.

[1] Dr. Aveling has published an account of a conversation with my father. I think that the readers of this pamphlet (*The Religious Views of Charles Darwin*, Free Thought Publishing Company, 1883) may be misled into seeing more resemblance than really existed between the positions of my father and Dr. Aveling : and I say this in spite of my conviction that Dr. Aveling gives quite fairly his impressions of my father's views. Dr. Aveling tried to show that the terms " Agnostic " and " Atheist " were practically equivalent— that an atheist is one who, without denying the existence of God, is without God, inasmuch as he is unconvinced of the existence of a Deity. My father's replies implied his preference for the unaggressive attitude of an Agnostic. Dr. Aveling seems (p. 5) to regard the absence of aggressiveness in my father's views as distinguishing them in an unessential manner from his own. But, in my judgment, it is precisely differences of this kind which distinguish him so completely from the class of thinkers to which Dr. Aveling belongs.

THE FORUM SERIES

Each volume bound in clothette at 1s. net (by post 1s. 2d.),
and in paper cover at 7d. net (by post 8d.).

THE STREAM OF LIFE.
By Professor JULIAN S. HUXLEY.

Manchester Guardian.—" It would be hard to find a better or more stimulating introduction to the general study of biology."

THE RELIGION OF AN ARTIST.
By the Hon. JOHN COLLIER.

Nation and Athenæum.—" It could hardly be improved."

MR. BELLOC OBJECTS TO " THE OUTLINE OF HISTORY."
By H. G. WELLS.

An acute and masterly criticism.

THE GOODNESS OF GODS.
By EDWARD WESTERMARCK, Ph.D.

Dr. Westermarck wields a facile pen, and he has never used it to greater effect than he has done in this delightful work.

CONCERNING MAN'S ORIGIN.
By Professor Sir ARTHUR KEITH.

The Presidential Address to the British Association, 1927 (with additions), and other Essays.

THE EARTH : ITS NATURE AND HISTORY.
By EDWARD GREENLY, D.Sc., F.G.S.

Sheffield Daily Telegraph.—" For the beginner in the science of geology it is one of the most useful books yet published."

CRAFTSMANSHIP AND SCIENCE.
By Professor WILLIAM H. BRAGG.

The Presidential Address to the British Association, 1928, with supplementary Essays.

DARWINISM AND WHAT IT IMPLIES.
By Professor Sir ARTHUR KEITH.

Contains the famous Ludwig Mond lecture, dealing with Immortality.

WHAT IS EUGENICS ?
By Major LEONARD DARWIN.

A comprehensive exposition, including a chapter on Birth Control.

THE MEANING OF LIFE, AS SHOWN IN THE PROCESS OF EVOLUTION. By C. E. M. JOAD.

A subtle and powerful exposition of Vitalism.

London : WATTS & CO., Johnson's Court, Fleet Street, E.C.4.